First Printing, 2012
ISBN-13: 978-1478316343
ISBN-10: 1478316349
www.frankbuytendijk.com

Socrates Reloaded

The Case for Ethics in Business & Technology

Frank Buytendijk

beingfrank

Table of contents

Introduction

What would the old philosophers have said about modern themes in business and IT?

Technology innovation is about lifting constraints and eliminating boundaries. For example, smartphones have amazing computing power, yet are small enough to fit in a pocket. The Internet renders distance irrelevant. Analytical tools process unimaginable amounts of information in no time. The cloud solves issues of storage. And so forth.

With so much technology innovation in such a short period of time, the questions that business and technology professionals wrestle with move from "How do we do things?" (within the boundaries of technology) to "What do we do with all that power?"

Once you realize this, it seems there are more questions in modern business than answers. Are there any ethical limits in integrating and analyzing all the information we have? Who owns the data that our customers share with us? How do we judge if all the business technology we have at our disposal does what is right? How do modern technologies affect our lives? Will technology make our lives and businesses better? How should we define what "better" really means? How do we govern the use of technology in business?

These are confusing times, as the cliché goes.
In confusing times, there is only one safe place to turn to for answers. To yourself. Take a deep look inside yourself to understand what you really stand for, what you believe in and what you think is the right way forward.

This journey to yourself is an exercise in philosophy. Scary or even esoteric as this may sound, it is not. Philosophy certainly not restricted to university campuses and PhDs. This book is the living proof. It is a series of practical, provocative, playful and easy-to-read essays that meander through different branches of philosophy throughout history. These essays share a common theme: What would the old philosophers have said about modern themes in business and IT? Or in slightly hipper terms: "Socrates Reloaded."

It's an ideal theme indeed. It allows me to speculate wildly on a number of topics, and put words in the mouths of people who have been dead for hundreds of years (at least most of them). What are they going to do? Slap me on the fingers? Unlikely.

Although the essays are light, I am serious about what I write and what I intend to achieve. The essays parallel my journey to determine where I stand. That journey has now led to five books with hopefully many more to come. What I hope these essays can do for you, dear reader, is make you stop and think. Question the best practices you've been using and the principles you've been following. Look at things from a different perspective, choose a different angle. Put yourself in the shoes of someone you don't agree with, and see things from that side.

All essays in this book try to provide a new angle, a different perspective. Perhaps you agree, and you gain an additional perspective. Perhaps you don't agree and feel even stronger about the beliefs you already had.

In fact, I hope you disagree. I'd like you to argue with me because then we both learn. Approaching interesting questions and topics from different points of view has a long tradition. Socrates was most famous for that. He would walk through Athens, in search of wisdom, asking questions of people in important positions – "what-if analysis" we would call it today.

Where do I stand?

Philosophers throughout the ages rarely agreed. For each view, there has been at least one opposing view, and these views are discussed endlessly. For me, finding out where I stand has been a surprisingly automatic process. It's not that doing the research for the essays taught me what to think about issues. It has been more the other way around. The research taught me the theory that explained my natural thinking, and has taught me adjacent and opposing views so I could give my thoughts, beliefs and ideas a place.

Looking back, the central influence in most of my research, and certainly in my books, has been the importance of the stakeholder view on business. Stakeholders are parties who benefit from our success, who'd like to see us do well. They have needs that we need to address, but also unique contributions to make. One doesn't go without the other. Stakeholders in business include customers, staff, suppliers, investors, governing institutions and society at large.

In writing my third book, *Performance Leadership*[1], I came to the conclusion that the common definition of an organization – a group of people sharing the same goal – didn't work for me. It seemed to me more the cause of a number of problems I saw than the vision of how to build a focused company. I learned that from a stakeholder point of view, an organization is a unique collaboration of people who need each other to accomplish their own goals.

That was the starting point for the fourth book, *Dealing with Dilemmas*[2], in which I argue that strategic management is about understanding stakeholder requirements and reconciling their differences. Strategy is dealing with dilemmas, which requires synthesis as opposed to what we learn in school and in business, namely analysis. I learned that stakeholder-centric decision making requires a deep understanding of underlying moral aspects. Ethics and morality are important topics in philosophy, and I decided to make that the next object of study, leading to the book that you are reading now.

In writing the essays composing this book, I found myself returning to stakeholder-oriented solutions. I found a stakeholder view is often missing in enterprise architecture. I found that governance discussions were often structured top-down. They were dominated by the management perspective instead of an understanding of a

1 Buytendijk, F.A., 2008, Performance Leadership: The Next Practices to Motivate Your People, Align Stakeholders and Lead Your Industry, McGraw-Hill
2 Buytendijk, F.A., 2010, Dealing with Dilemmas: Where Business Analytics Fall Short, Wiley & Sons

force at least as powerful – the power of being governed.

Another big topic that needs attention because of technology innovation is "ethics." Decisions in business directly affect society. Broadly, there are two schools of thought in philosophy. There are universalists who believe that we can define universal principles of ethics and determine upfront what is good or bad. All we need to do then is to follow those principles. Always. No exceptions. Perhaps a modern term for these people would be "hardliners."

Then there are the consequentialists. They believe that the consequences of our actions determine whether these actions were good or bad. We can only determine this after the fact. Killing a person to save the lives of many others can be justified this way.

Similarly, companies downplaying in the press how bad they are doing in order to save jobs can also be justified this way. Transparency, consequentalists claim, is not always a good thing.

Somehow, for me, both ends don't work. Consequentialism is just too easy. It creates an external locus of control, and it doesn't provide a moral compass at all. Not very helpful. At the same time, the universalist approach is just too rigid. "Sorry, I just followed the rules" is not a very strong argument when you are challenged on the moral implications of a decision you made. Not personally, and not in business. As we are social beings, it is not about creating the best set of moral principles and rules, but making sure we have the best possible society. That requires a certain flexibility because our ideas of what "best possible" means change over time. We improve as we go. Hopefully.

What disqualifies both approaches for me is that as human beings, we are deeply flawed. We moved beyond the idea of the *homo economicus* from the Age of Reason. People have bounded rationality, as economist and sociologist Herbert Simon noted. We have serious cognitive limitations. We cannot really oversee the consequences of our decisions and actions, and judge if they are good or bad from all different perspectives. And as we are all products of our own times, we definitely can't claim universal truth.

If the consequentialist and universalist approaches to ethics don't work for me, what does work? First and foremost, I think universalism and consequentialism are not opposites. They can be perfectly reconciled through the point of view of us being non (or less-) rational beings. I think we display our ethical behavior *principally* in how we *deal with consequences*. How do we react when we are faced with unintended consequences of our actions? What do we do when things don't work out? How do we correct mistakes? How do we reflect on our own behavior when we don't truly understand what we do?

In business terms, can we fail fast? Can we admit early on that we made a mistake and correct it without playing the "blame game"? Or do we fall in the trap of not understanding "sunk cost," unable to pull the plug on initiatives that we know will fail?

Can we share success? Are we able to identify all stakeholders that contribute to our success and set up a business model and reward system that benefits all? Or do we treat business as a zero-sum game and keep all returns for ourselves in this "dog-eat-dog" world?

Can we generously apologize and compensate stakeholders when needed? Sometimes making mistakes disadvantages others as well. Sometimes we need to do a product recall. How do we balance moral and legal aspects of such an operation?

Do we accept honest criticism and feedback and take it to heart? Do we listen to people around us who mean well? Do we recognize people who have a passion for success, and do we allow them to tell us the things we don't want to hear? Or do we suspect they have a hidden agenda or believe there is nothing we can learn from others about business?

Those are the measures of an ethical person, and an ethical business.

Thank you!

You can't write a book in isolation. At least, I can't. This book is the result of countless interactions with many people. A big thank you also goes to Christopher Welge, PhD candidate at the University of Würzburg, Germany, for all the heated debates and his thorough review. The same applies to Arnoud van Gemeren as well, editor-in-chief of TITM (Magazine for IT Management in The Netherlands), who reminded me that writing is about killing your darlings. Ramon van der Aa and Claudette Kints, thank you for being my test readers. Furthermore, I'd like to thank, in alphabetical order, Jaap Bloem, Axel Brink, Alcedo Coenen, Gary Cokins, Willem Dicou, Esther Doller, Jan Willem Ebbinge, Thei Geurts, Art Lighthart, Dick van Mersbergen and Hotze Zijlstra for their valuable comments, directions and discussions. Special thanks go to Rick van der Lans and Emiel van Bockel. It was in a brainstorm meeting with them that I decided to write a book on philosophy and technology.

For a book to be successful, it shouldn't only read well; it should also look good. Andy Bitterer is the most gifted photographer that I know, and I would like to thank him for designing the cover of the book. Danielle Westerhout and Mathieu Westerveld, both at ICT Media, thank you for all the help with the book's layout and getting it published.

I'd also like to thank Jean Schauer and Kerry Flood, editors at BeyeNETWORK (www.b-eye-network.com) for all their encouragement and help polishing these essays.

Most of all, I would like to thank all the attendees at conferences around the world for listening to and participating in my keynotes and workshops. You patiently let me try material and sharpen my saw. You came up with many examples that have proven to be very useful. I hope you'll find them reflected in the book.

Frank Buytendijk
Twitter: @FrankBuytendijk
Email: f.a.buytendijk@planet.nl

IT:
Information
Technology
or
Independent
Thinking...

Interesting
Thought!

How many philosophers does it take to change a light bulb?

Erm... What exactly does it mean
to be a light bulb?
And... what exactly does it mean to mean something?
What exactly is exactly?
What???

It is easy to dismiss philosophy as impractical and an unnecessary luxury, particularly because the world is changing faster and faster. We have no time to sit and have beautiful thoughts because before we know it reality has overtaken us. Actions speak louder than words. Musings on how things could, should and would be in a perfect world are better discussed in front of the fireplace or with your therapist.

But is this really true? Are globalization, the astonishing rate of change, and progress of technology not all the more reason to take the time to reflect? It is so easy to lose yourself, rushing from one priority to the next. In the book *Seven Habits of Highly Effective People*, Stephen Covey observes a man frantically busy trying to saw wood while a bystander remarks that he should probably sharpen his saw first. The man responds, slightly irritated: "No time! Can't you see I am busy sawing wood?" Covey uses the term "sharpening the saw" as a metaphor for reflection, which in turn leads to better, faster work. Philosophy sharpens the saw.

Every profession has its own philosophy. There's political philosophy, medical philosophy, legal philosophy, religious philosophy, scientific philosophy and so forth. There is also a branch called philosophy of technology, but during a brief moment of popularity, it was dominated by cyberpunks and futurists. Somehow philosophy is not very popular in the IT industry. Most IT educations do not teach philosophy, and in many organizations philosophical questions remain unanswered.

That is odd, to say the least, because IT professionals

and philosophers have a lot in common. Both professions are focused on thinking things through, and using analysis to understand the essence and working of things. IT people, for instance, speak of functional decomposition to describe all elements of an envisioned system. Both professions have a very conceptual and logical view on the world, which is another reason it is strange that IT people do not have more appreciation for philosophy. Wasn't it Socrates who laid a lot of the groundwork for today's logic, rivaled only much later by Spinoza, Heidegger and Russell? Weren't Euclid, Pythagoras and Descartes some of the main contributors to mathematics?

IT professionals, like most philosophers, enjoy discussing definitions at their leisure. There are endless debates on what *cloud computing* or *enterprise 2.0* really means, and these debates are not likely to get resolved soon. In fact, IT professionals have been arguing for the last twenty years about what the exact definition is of *business intelligence* and *knowledge management*, for example. Maybe these endless debates are caused by the conceptual nature of IT. I mean, have you ever heard two greengrocers debate how to define an orange? I haven't!

As in philosophy, in IT there always multiple – often conflicting – schools of thought. One group of IT professionals prefers one view, while the other group holds an opposing thought, such as in data or process modeling. Having multiple schools of thought is not unique; it happens in every conceptual discipline, like macroeconomics (e.g., how to deal with a crisis) and strategy (Henry Mintzberg even defines ten distinct schools of thought).

Both professions are known for their ability to create frameworks and models to describe reality and to share certain views. Think of different frameworks to describe an enterprise architecture, a project management methodology or something like function point analysis to estimate the complexity of certain project. These frameworks come with a lot of jargon, another commonality between IT and philosophy. Why are these difficult terms needed?

Actually, jargon is part of every profession. Doctors have jargon and so do carpenters. There is a need for jargon – not (just) to create an aura of wisdom, but to be able to concisely and precisely communicate. Although medical jargon may be relatively precise, IT jargon certainly is not. Many terms are very ill-defined. Think, again, of *cloud computing*, or of *software/process/everything-as-a-service*. This may be a clear difference from philosophy, as philosophers do not have the luxury of marketing departments seeking to differentiate from the competition.

Another similarity is that both IT professionals and philosophers tend to position themselves slightly outside of reality, like commentators. IT people frequently refer to the rest of the organization they work for as "the business," while philosophers talk about "life" and "society" as if they weren't part of them. Both professions feel that taking an abstract view positions themselves above the matter they discuss. It gives them oversight, insight and provides them with a deeper understanding. Some IT people go as far as to call themselves *business architects*.

At the same time, there are many differences between IT professionals and philosophers; most noticeably, IT people get paid better. Just never claim that philosophy is not practical. Aristotle wrote about Thales (c. 624-547 BC), one of the first known Greek philosophers, physicists and mathematicians, who during winter read from the weather and the stars that the next year would have a great olive harvest. He made a fortune by buying up all the olive-presses he could get his hands on and renting them out when it was harvest time.[1]

Why is (IT) Philosophy Important?

Philosophy is the attempt to solve the mysteries of being through thinking. Philosophy helps us understand

---

1 At the same time, Plato shares a story about how Thales walks into a ditch while looking into the sky, and is mocked by a peasant girl: "How can you understand what happens in the sky, if you don't even see what is at your feet?"

ourselves, the world and the relationship between the two. It is in people's natures to look for explanations of events, whether good or bad. In fact, you could call this the basis of religious philosophy. Some find consolation in their belief in God – everything happens for a higher reason. Others find strength in the idea that life is the result of random evolution and that there is no ultimate explanation of things happening to us.

Plato wrote that Socrates said philosophy is a necessary component in obtaining wisdom and knowledge. Without it, how can you agree or disagree with someone else? How can you question anything you hear, see, read or experience? If you don't examine yourself and your environment, you don't learn, you don't see your own or someone else's mistakes, you can't explain what is happening around you and, most probably, you end up just kidding yourself. Without philosophy, Socrates basically argued, life would be boring, consisting only of simple positions – i.e., black and white, right and wrong – instead of rich gray areas.

Philosophy, first of all, teaches you how to think. It teaches you how to judge a line of argument, evaluate objections and reason in a logical way. In the words of Socrates, "If I can follow good arguments wherever they lead, then my thinking perhaps improves, and I may reduce the degree to which I fool myself." Concepts such as deduction and induction were derived from philosophy. Deduction is the process of taking a general idea or rule and applying it to certain circumstances, while induction is the opposite approach: collecting as many observations as possible on a certain phenomenon, and trying to create an overall theory that explains all observations.[2]

It is practical to know when to apply which style of

---

2 Although induction and deduction are really Logic 101, it is easy to get it wrong. For instance, Sherlock Holmes is famous for saying "Deduction, my dear Watson," where you could argue in the end detective work is inductive of nature, using small details to unravel the mystery.

thinking. For instance, applying a methodology for building a business case is deductive of nature, while requirements gathering requires inductive thinking. Although IT people are often strong conceptual thinkers, studying philosophy would help them stand on the shoulders of giants.

Second, philosophy teaches you there are different ways of thinking and each way might be equally logical and convincing. Mathematicians will claim that 1+1=2, and that it is hard to argue with that. An organizational theorist might add that in his world, 1+1 sometimes equals 3, introducing the idea of synergy. If two elements each have a characteristic that strengthens a characteristic of the other part, the value of the whole may be bigger than the sum of its parts. If one person has design skills, and the other knows how to program, together they can build a well-functioning system, something they could not have done on their own. Physicists may add the example of nitroglycerine, and biologists would chime in reminding us of the process of procreation.

Different ways of thinking can be equally true, but may be adopted by different schools of thought. Another business example may be the competing factions in organizational goal setting. One school of thought is that the ultimate goal of every business is to create and optimize shareholder value, as the business is owned by its shareholders. Another school of thought reasons the goal of an organization is to sustain itself, like every other mechanism, so it should focus on stakeholder value, and profits are merely the oxygen of the organization. Both types of logic are hard to disqualify.

Third, once you understand there are multiple ways of thinking, you can examine and question your own thinking as well. Preconceptions you may have held for a long time may not hold up, and you may have to change your fundamental beliefs as a consequence. This can be unsettling, but leads to a higher level of thinking: meta-thinking. Philosophy helps you think about how you think.

Once you master that, or at least apply it, your results are more creative and multidimensional of nature and you've been able to test your ideas against multiple views and scenarios.

It is surprisingly hard to accept that you can separate a person from his or her ideas, though. The story of Carneades confirms this. Carneades, heading the Academy that was founded by Plato in 385 B.C., was sent on a mission to Rome in 156 B.C., and he decided to combine the mission with a series of lectures. Because Greek philosophy was popular in Rome in those days, there was a lot of interest. During the first lecture, Carneades explained the views of Aristotle and Plato, which people were thrilled to hear. In the second lecture, Carneades reasoned the complete opposite and was equally convincing. The point was not to prove Aristotle and Plato wrong, but to show the skeptics that there are different ways of thinking. This caused consternation among Roman politicians, especially senator Marcus Cato, who felt this independent thinking was a bad influence on Rome's youth. Instead, he complained to the senate that it was better for the people to simply obey the law. As a result, Carneades was sent home.

Fast forward to the 21st century; surely, we have progressed. A few years ago, I participated in what we called a "dialectical debate" as a keynote at a large conference. My co-presenter, Wayne Eckerson, currently research director at TechTarget, and I came up with the idea of taking opposing views in reaction to propositions from the moderator of the conference. Then we would switch sides and equally vigorously argue the opponent's view, bringing new arguments to the table. We even visualized it by holding up red or green cards to indicate if we were arguing for or against. Although the attendees were amused (at least that improved in two millennia), they were still confused. They insisted that we share what we *really* believed. What did we believe? Well, all of it!

Finally, once you understand how to think, that there are multiple ways of thinking, and that you can master multiple ways, philosophy helps you communicate better. When thinking things through, include the most obvious objections or different viewpoints, making it easier for others to buy into your line of argumentation. You will then be able to explain your message clearly, logically and persuasively.

Why is IT philosophy important *now*?

We cannot imagine a world without IT anymore. "I think there is a world market for about five computers," is one of the most famously wrong predictions in history.[3] Computers are all around us, and with sensor networks and an endless choice of computerized devices the online world and the real world are inextricably intertwined. There is really no such thing as pure business IT anymore. Business systems are used by customers to make their lives easier, e.g., self-service airline check-in or Internet banking. Employees bring their own devices and computers to the office. Business technology is consumerized, and consumer technology is used in business. IT is not only the backbone of business, but the backbone of society. In some countries, governments have declared the ability to go online as a basic necessity of life.

At the same time, to reference another cliche, technology advancements still seem to continue at an exponential pace. Moore's Law – that computer capacity doubles every two years – remains valid for the years to come.

This exponential growth and scalability, both in terms of number of users as well as pure capacity, means that the questions we ask ourselves before embarking on an IT initiative need to change. Long gone are the days of asking "what" to do with IT. In fact, the question of "how" to do things becomes less and less relevant as well, as many of the constraints that triggered those questions are simply lifted. The question that becomes really important is

---

3 This quote is often attributed to Thomas Watson, a former CEO of IBM, but it is unclear if he truly said this.

"Why?" If everything is possible, having a clue on why to do things is the only way to set priorities and think through the consequences of our choices.

Asking yourself why to do things is a question of philosophy. It requires an understanding of what you believe in. Do you, for instance, believe that IT is a means of controlling life (or business for that matter) and reducing uncertainties? Then indeed, one of the first applications to download on your new PDA would be a location-based system to track known criminals in your neighborhood, and you might frown on allowing people to use Facebook in the workplace. If you believe IT is supposed to liberate people from unnecessary labor and is fundamentally a means of collaboration and communication, then Facebook might be the first application you'll set up on your new device.

The "why" question is not new in technology. Stem cell researchers have been wrestling with the question for years, and still do. The arguments for are as equally convincing as the arguments against. The military faced the dilemma of whether to allow public use of the GPS system, balancing the clear advantages against the perceived risks of such available technology. Any IT used in business or in society can be used in the wrong way as well. Fingerprint data stored in a database to prevent passport fraud may also be used for other purposes. Integrated electronic patient files can be used by insurance companies to exclude customers. Scanning license plates on the highway to collect tolls can also be used to track people. Through centralized data centers – to which we have outsourced all our pictures, blogs, documents, and voicemails – others have potential access to all our dreams, thoughts, communications, and so forth. All of a sudden, George Orwell's 1984 is not that far away.

Whenever technological boundaries are lifted, new moral and ethical dilemmas emerge. Should new and powerful technologies be forbidden, regulated or restricted to ensure they don't fall into the wrong hands or get used in the wrong way? Or should we accept negative consequences because of the overwhelmingly positive impact that new technologies could have?

Out of the 100 largest economic entities in the world, more than one third are corporations, not countries. Business has a social responsibility as well. In order to live up to that responsibility, CIOs should be prepared to engage in moral debate today.

What Does it Take To Be an IT Philosopher?

Go figure, the philosophers actually don't agree on what it takes to be a philosopher. Plato despised the "sophists" that were merely interested in cunning debate; he believed a true philosopher should not have any interest in worldly matters and instead focus on higher purposes, such as what constitutes truth and beauty. More recently, Heidegger felt that philosophical discussions should be for the highest of educated people. Using lots of difficult words and jargon is a just barrier, a self-selection mechanism. Only the ones capable of mastering the jargon were worthy of true philosophy. But only in the last few centuries have the philosophers been academics.

Philosophy literally means "the love for wisdom." You don't need to have a PhD[4] in philosophy to love wisdom. In fact, British philosopher and publicist Brian Magee observes that nearly always some of the best practitioners in any field are interested in its philosophy and understanding its fundamental issues. I think it works both ways. If you are among the best IT practitioners, you (re)discover the most fundamental questions, such as "What is strategy?", "What is an organization?" or "What is technology?" But conversely, asking yourself these questions and trying to find the answers based on what others have said before, as well as figuring out what you believe in, makes you a better practitioner. Improving as an IT practitioner means asking yourself differ-

---

4 In fact, PhD actually stands for doctor of philosophy, in contrast to MD, which is a doctor of medicine.

ent questions throughout your career anyway.

First of all, you need to have the "know what" and learn the ropes of the trade. What is it that you need to do in certain situations, following best practices? Building expertise leads to the "know how," in which you learn variations on best practices and also know how to let them go, as reading the situation gives you the right answers already. Last comes the "know why, "the domain of philosophy. This allows you to work on the metalevel, understanding the purpose of different approaches, concepts and technologies.

Obviously the "know why" is complex, and the road to these questions can be long. Some concepts simply are complex and hard to understand the first time you encounter them. That is why they need to be explained and taught well. But this is not different than studying any other subject, such as economy, mathematics or French. Compare it with becoming a sushi chef. You start with the basics, cutting the cucumber or cooking the rice. Over the years, moving from the "know what" via the "know how" to the "know why," you become a sushi master and can return to the basics, cooking rice and cutting cucumber. It's full circle, but what a difference in context! You now understand the tools you use, the structure of your ingredients, and even the literal chemistry of combining ingredients.

Reading about the great philosophers and trying to apply those lessons to IT doesn't have to be intimidating. The history of philosophy shows that many build on top of each other's work, which means after thousands of years there is a lot to build on. And philosophy has changed the last few hundred years, too. The most famous philosophers are known for their huge new ideas, sweeping schools of thought and building complete systems of thinking. Today, our understanding of the world in all its complexity and interconnectivity often makes philosophy a discussion of smaller topics, and can be empirical of nature. In other words, simply taking situations as they appear and thinking through their consequences, which is what we are trained to do as IT professionals.

That is why we attend conferences, are members of professional organizations, and create frameworks used to explain complex concepts, as philosophers do.

So ... how many philosophers does it take to change a light bulb?

Nine.

One to change the light bulb, and the other eight to discuss how Nietzsche would have done it.

Did Marx Predict the End of The Internet Giants?

Since the credit crunch of 2008, sales of Karl Marx' book Das Kapital ("Capital") has more than tripled. Publisher Schütrumpf ordered a new edition, 4000 copies, with the printer. "Although for large publishers these are small numbers, you should realize this is one of the most complex scientific publications of the last 200 years," Schütrumpf says.

Marx? I can almost hear you thinking, Marx?? As Marx is associated with communism, he is often regarded as a figure from the past, and the relevance is lost. However, since the 2008 credit crunch, Marx seems to be back on the main stage. Many commentators have pointed out that in his book *Das Kapital* (1867), he predicted the financial crisis through his analysis of the consequences of unbridled capitalism.

Everyone is a product of his or her own time, and Marx is no exception. Karl Marx (1818-1883) was born in Germany, lived in France and later moved to England. The German influence in Marx' work comes from Georg Wilhelm Friedrich Hegel and is represented through Marx' description of how reality is a continuously changing historical process, based on action, reaction and synthesis between the two. Change is inevitable and moves according to its own laws. It is not under control by human beings. Understanding these forces of change is key to understanding reality. Marx was a revolutionary, undoubtedly fueled by his upbringing in Trier, Germany, after the French revolution of 1789. And Marx was very much influenced by the English Industrial Revolution and the society with classes, such the blue-collar working class and the white-collar upper class. This makes Marx' philosophy an economical one.

The Road to Communism

Marx thought of his work as scientific, uncovering the laws of economics and the circumstances in society that drive change. Socialism and communism were inevitable. These ideas had a huge following, and several states were built on these ideas; but, in general, events have not played out the way Marx had predicted them. Until...the credit crunch of 2008. The similarities of the credit crunch and the following recession to Marx' description of the downfall of capitalism are striking.

My interpretation of Marx' argument[1] goes something like this. If you invest capital in a factory that produces goods, you add value, basically the difference between the revenue and the cost of production, such as wages, materials and so forth. The added value lands in the wallets of just a few capitalists and not in the hands of the many workers who produced the goods. The profits enable more investments and lead to more profits (it seems the aspect of entrepreneurial risk was less emphasized). In the words of Marx: "The chief motive of capitalism is greed, and the war amongst the greedy is called competition." In the war of the greedy to grow and accumulate wealth, large corporations start to swallow the small ones. In the quest for wealth, profit margins need to increase, leading to longer work hours, lower wages, and a degradation in working conditions. Furthermore, the workforce is replaced by machines, as they are more efficient. This leads to higher unemployment rates. In short, the rich get richer and the poor get poorer.

Once the profit wheel starts to accelerate, not all profits can be reinvested in the company. To achieve higher returns on investment, these profits need to leave the real economy of factories and goods. Capital starts to flow to banks in order to invest and speculate as this leads to higher overall average returns, thereby meeting shareholder expectations, but inevitably also leading to the many "bubbles" that we have seen.

---

1 This represents my interpretation, and not my opinion. I neither agree nor disagree with Marx for the purpose of this series of articles; I simply needed to explain it to be able to describe my main point of the need for an information democracy.

So, at one moment, the poor cannot afford to consume anymore, leading to overproduction (as supply becomes bigger than demand) and to living on credit (to maintain a certain standard of living). Overproduction leads to companies folding, while at the same time as the poor get even poorer, they cannot pay off their debt. And when, as part of a perfect storm, an investment bubble bursts, there is a full-blown crisis. *Banks are the first to collapse.* They lose the securities and the money they have invested, and the government needs to step in—the first step toward socialism and inevitably communism.

Sound familiar? Perhaps the step to socialism isn't as inevitable as Marx described it. We haven't seen revolution and a battle of the classes, but the 2008 crisis did lead to society needing to get control over unbridled capitalism and to the questioning of many of the principles we had in place. In essence, it is a return to "pure" capitalism as it was meant by Adam Smith, where the "invisible hand" of the market did not mean that the market had to run itself (what the free market turned into), but was to be guided by moral and ethical considerations.

Have we learned something? Will capitalism getting out of control never happen again? I am not sure...

The Information Age: L'histoire se répète

Capital was the fuel of the economy in the industrial age. Now we live in the information age. Capital and information have a few things in common. Information is a factor of production, like labor, materials, facilities and capital. Without information you cannot run an organization. Information is the engine of today's economic growth. The person with the best information about what is happening in the market has an advantage over the others. Capital comes second, and draws to the people with the best information, such as venture capitalists. Information suffers from inflation as well. We seem to want more and more information to satisfy our needs. I should point out that there are also differences. Information is not as liquid as capital is. You can't exchange information based on a common standard of value. There are no established exchange rates. And, in theory, capital is a scarce good, while information is not. It can be duplicated without significant effort and consequence. However, before the economic crisis, capital was abundantly available as well (in search for a higher rate of profit). The lack of scarcity may even amplify the need for greed, in order to increase one's share of the growing pie.

Furthermore, and this makes the argument of the information age mimicking the industrial age even stronger, information has a much shorter half-life than money. If it is not used in time, it often loses value.

But the most important comparison between capital and information comes from a pure human characteristic, greed. Are we as greedy for information as we are for money? Looking at the operating practices of the Internet giants, it seems so.[2] They are continuously looking for more and more information in order to grow their businesses. Their business models are mostly based on advertisement revenue, which in itself is an information product as well.

A critical success factor for a Web search engine, is to accumulate as much Web information as possible to make sure that it can accurately respond to search requests from users. But there is a flying wheel effect. The more searches users trust to a search engine, the more the engine learns about what users are looking for. This is not only interesting feedback to users in terms of optimized search results, but also to customers who place their advertisements. The ability to provide customers with more precisely placed

---

2 The Internet giants include the popular social networks, search engines, review websites and openly accessible databases. Most of them have the same business model: "free" to use, paid by advertisers. They have hundreds of millions of users, often billions of revenue. Their sheer size and influence almost force you to use them. Wikipedia is an Internet giant that is an exception, still based on volunteer work and volunteer monetary contributions.

advertisements results in happier customers—and a happier search engine provider.

Internet giants want to be more than just a place to look things up, or chat with each other. Many want to be the central place where we go for any information exchange, *like a bank*. Today, Internet giants control our mobile phones, our Web-based calls, some of our browsers, our email, and our collaboration platforms. They have permeated the popular trading platforms with analytics software and possibilities to share what you buy with friends. Soon they will cross over to "real-life," when "augmented reality" devices will provide real-time information on everything you see, hear and witness.

The Internet giants have caused many a stir already, around copyrights of books, music, movies and other traditional information carriers. In one example, an email provider even proposed targeted advertising based on analyzing email subjects and texts. Providers of geographic information (maps) got in trouble by collecting too much information when taking pictures of every street, or taking pictures of people who objected.

As happened with manufacturing companies in the 19th century, it will take considerable time before the Internet giants find a balance to meet the needs of all stakeholders. There is no reason to believe that Internet giants, hungry for information, are different from shareholder-driven firms, hungry for capital.

In their hunger for more data to feed their customers (the advertisers), the Internet giants are redefining what privacy means. This will continue to create scandals, and cause harm to people and society for the foreseeable future. Until the next scandal.

Indeed, Marx would have been quick to point out a few parallels to the industrial age. Internet companies have a greed for more information, just as there was greed for more capital in the industrial age. And collecting more information allows you to generate more information. Marx probably would have spotted a divide between the information haves and the information have-nots. Social tension! Even the exploitation dynamic is the same: the information is not collected for the best interest of the users. In fact, the users are not the real customers. The information is collected for the best interest of the shareholders and the real customers; the advertisers. Marx might even have pointed at the tendency to simply store everything you can find and opening all information by default. He might have called it overproduction. A revolution in the making!

So the data-rich get richer, but how do the data-poor get poorer? Search engines and social networks actually deliver true added value for the users: excellent ways of finding information and capabilities to maintain friendships across many borders. Don't they? Furthermore, one could argue that the so-called exploitation is entirely self-inflicted. Users willfully visit the search engines and social network sites because they simply are not willing to pay for the services these sites provide free of charge. Because search engines and social networks are run by commercial companies, their profits need to come from elsewhere: selling advertising space based on the careful analysis of personal data.

However, as the data-rich get richer and as their footprint expands, the users start to increasingly depend on the use of their services. Truth is that the data-rich already do everything in their power to make the users as dependent as possible. Have you ever tried to close a social media account? The providers will hit every emotional button to try to convince you to stay. It will show a screen with pictures of your friends, telling you how much they will miss you. And if you are persistent, there is no easy way to bring your data with you. It's basically gone... well, it is in the archive for further analysis.

Marx's writings actually provide for the argument that users inflict privacy issues on themselves. We can draw a parallel between the use of the Internet and what Marx called the "opium of the people": religion. He called religion the opium of the people, not for the people, as the people created religion themselves to create a feeling of well-being in an unbearable world. All will be better in the afterlife, but for the time being the people will remain exploited and ignorant. As soon as the people would take control, religion would not be needed anymore. Free use of information—for the time being—and all the triggers in place to want more and more to satisfy the growing needs is the opium of the people today. The chance to look at video clips and to chat with our friends online keeps us happy. We choose to be dependent on Internet giants; we choose to be exploited by demanding the services for free. Think about it, we do it to ourselves. It sounds para-doxical: by demanding free service, we let ourselves be exploited. Only once we start paying for "free" Internet services, we become customers of the company with legit-imate expectations. Until then, we choose to be exploited.

Marx would also have been the first to say that all the ingredients for a revolt are there. What could happen to In-ternet giants if they shoot themselves in the feet by push-ing their data collection and analysis too far? Not neces-sarily bloodshed, but a multitude of things could happen in the 21st century. The government could step in and impose rules, or even split up the company. In fact, regu-latory bodies, such as the FTC, have already been called into action examining default privacy settings. There's the power of the traditional media that could bring the In-ternet giants down, exposing scandals. In fact, in the in-formation age, oh irony, the public opinion, expressed by traditional media, is formed by using the very social net-works that need to be corrected. The fastest way to learn about new privacy settings on your social network usu-ally is through your social network contacts!

Then, as we still have an open market, there is always competition. If one company messes up, another will stand up and take its market share. Another – even hipper – provider might come in and leverage the power of com-munity, bringing in heaps of users through attracting just a few key users—that bring their networks. Other large companies may feel they have the power to withstand the Internet Giants and find a technological way to simply close their websites to searches. Smart users themselves may find ways to fight back, for instance by launching a technology that randomly responds to all kinds of ads, messing up profiles, and making the ad owners pay for no results. Or they can devise filters that mask your identity before visiting a search engine. In fact, there already is a "Web 2.0 Suicide Machine," a handy application that discontinues your accounts on all major social networks. What would take hours to do manually will be done in seconds by this application. The end of the data-hungry indeed.

Toward an Information Democracy

Returning to Marx, what will happen after that revolution? What new model will emerge? Adopting Hegelian dialectics (thesis-antithesis-synthesis), reaction will follow action over and over again until there is no longer any tension causing these reactions. As Marx saw the battle of the classes in the industrial age as the source of the tension, communism was his answer to eliminating tension. In a communistic society, all factors of production are owned by the people and put to use for the best interest of the people. In fact, there would be no need for a traditional government anymore (consisting of the upper class and suppressing the lower class); there would only be a need for a bureaucratic administration. How would that utopian view look in the world of information?

In fact, it already exists: Wikipedia, a free, web-based, collaborative, multilingual encyclopedia project supported by the non-profit Wikimedia Foundation. Wikipedia was launched in 2001 by Jimmy Wales and Larry Sanger, and currently contains more than 15 million articles in over 30 languages. Although disputed, an investigation in 2005 revealed that the accuracy of Wikipedia came close to the Encyclopaedia Brittanica. All content is created by the users, edited by the users, for the benefit of the users.

A very communistic view indeed. Even the terminology is the same, as instead of a government, Wikipedia is run by volunteering administrators.

We now know that the implementations of communism have been and are deeply flawed, becoming totalitarian and oppressive. Interestingly enough, Wikipedia is criticized for the same things.[3] The administrators of Wikipedia are accused of showing their own opinions, instead of simply administering the content creation process, and sometimes even argue with the most authoritative sources. Wikipedia's cofounder, Jimmy "Jimbo" Wales has a cult-like status among the administrators, who supposedly try to build power and gain appreciation from the leader by controlling more and more subject areas. In fact, the administrators have a great amount of control over the content, making Wikipedia much less open than it likes to portray itself.

Information Democracy

Marx was wrong. Society in and after the industrial age did not embrace communism. In fact, most of us live in democratic societies. Democracy comes from the Greek words *demos*, which means "people" and *krateo*, which means "power." In other words, "power to the people." Just not like Marx would have defined it. Democracies can be direct, where everyone has an equal vote in creating laws. Switzerland has a semi-direct democracy with its referenda, like some states in the United States as well. A parliamentary democracy, or indirect democracy, is more common. The people choose the representatives that decide over laws and govern the country on their behalf. The people still keep control, as the period for the mandate is limited, and is followed by new elections. An important aspect of Western democracies has been Montesquieu's trias politica, a separation of power into three: executive

---

3 It should be said though that an elaborate source for criticism on Wikipedia actually is a Wikipedia page

power by the government, legislative power by parliament and judicial power by the courts. Sometimes the media are called the fourth power.

So what about an information democracy? The term was used by Bill Gates, the then CEO of Microsoft, and by analyst firm Gartner for a while, but to my knowledge the term was never properly defined. There are as many views on democracy as there are people (which in itself is an important aspect of democracy), so it would be hard to make a definitive description of how an information democracy would look. However, examining the different aspects of a political democracy, information democracy at least it needs to be participative, governed, stakeholder-oriented, lateral and transparent.

In a democracy everyone has the right to speak up and initiate something to improve society, such as write to a congressman, start a petition or influence the public opinion. A democracy is *participative*, and so is an information democracy. Concepts such as "wisdom of crowds" are gaining popularity as an instrument for information democracy. "Wisdom of Crowds" (2004) is a book by James Surowiecki about the aggregation of information in groups, resulting in decisions that, he argues, are often better than could have been made by any single member of the group. If you ask many independent people for a prediction, the results are often remarkably close. Many people should have access to relevant information, should be able to discuss it, and should be able to challenge the results. If access to information is restricted to just a few, there is information elitism. It seems the Internet giants are doing pretty well in this regard. In fact, participation is the key to Everything 2.0.

To avoid information anarchy, where everyone is just creating their own information in their own way and where sharing is not the default, an information democracy should be *governed* well. Here, the Internet world can learn from more traditional business models. One can hardly call the hacker collective Anonymous a democratic functioning body. They may aim to protect Internet freedom, and fiercely attack anyone threatening that, but as they are anonymous, they are not transparent in what they do, can't be voted away, and can only be marginally influenced by society. In fact, I find their approach more totalitarian in nature. Wikipedia is already one step better. It is governed by the administrators, but with dysfunctional side effects. Wikipedia would benefit from a more formal peer review system, where the role of the administrators is limited to seeing that due process is followed (one critic called the administrators "fiercely territorial").

Or it could copy the model of the Stanford Encyclopedia of Philosophy, where entries are moderated by experts in their field. Social networks would benefit from an indirect democracy, in the form of a users council, where new functionalities and settings are tested first. Standardization has only just started on the Internet and within organizations for information management. The key is to organize the data using metadata, which describes the meaning of data. In the Internet world, this is called "Semantic Web." It improves the interoperability of information and even allows information exchange to be automated.

Whether an information democracy should be *stakeholder-oriented* can be disputed. Democracy in Western Europe is very much influenced by the utilitarian philosophers from England who coined the principle "the greatest good for the greatest number of people." In other words, one of the keys of a democracy is that the requirements of as many stakeholders as possible are taken into account when making decisions. In an information democracy, it means you would always look for ways to share information with multiple stakeholders, and express your success in terms of the success of the others as well. In the United States, "life, liberty and the pursuit of happiness" is the creed of its democracy, which is more individualistic. In an information democracy, this approach means everyone can get the information that he or she personally requires (Would this be information capitalism?). Taking a stakeholder view, some music providers are already beyond the advertising model. The service can be used for free, but then the true stakeholders are the customers that pay to place their advertisements. If you pay a certain monthly fee, use of more complete services is cleared from any advertisements. As a paying user equals a customer, stakeholder requirements are much more aligned.

Lateral information exchange means people can share and discuss information among each other. You can compare it to the freedom to congregate that modern democracies have. If lateral information exchange is not possible, there is information communism, where all information is determined by the top and simply cascaded through the hierarchy, like everything in a command economy (also known as centrally planned economy). It is ironic that modern enterprise, the hallmark of capitalism, is actually organized as a centrally planned economy when it comes to information management. The key performance indicators reflect the corporate goals, and alignment means nothing other than that all parts of the organization understand their contribution to those goals. Even if managers would be interested in the contribution of the others, or in what they contribute to the success of others, the reporting structures would not easily permit that insight. Organizations still have a lot of improvement potential here. However, social networks do nothing but facilitate lateral information exchange. Search usually is a more individualistic user experience. Seen this way, Wikipedia isn't democratic at all. Sure, there are conversations and there is some openness about debates behind Wikipedia articles, but contributors can all be anonymous.

Lastly, in an information democracy there should be *transparency*, like the media ensures in a political democracy. It should be clear where information is coming from and what is being done with it. Accountants would call this an audit trail. Although there is always rooms for improvement, in corporate life this is often taken care of relatively well. It is the Internet world that is actually lagging behind.

One more question is left: Is information democracy the nirvana of the information age? Here's the answer by Winston Churchill: "Many forms of Government have been tried and will be tried in this world of sin and woe. No one pretends that democracy is perfect or all-wise. Indeed, it has been said that democracy is the worst form of government except all those other forms that have been tried."

Medieval Best Practices

A young couple, just married, is preparing dinner. Before he puts the roast in the oven, he cuts it in two. She asks him why he is doing that, and he responds that this is how he was taught by his mother. That's how to prepare a roast. She is puzzled and suggests he call his mother. His mother's explanation? She always cut the roast in two because her oven was too small.

Enter the world of best practices, where we sometimes forget why we do things a certain way. Best practices is a commonly used term but the term's meaning is often unclear. If you search for a definition of best practices, the text books say that a best practice is a technique, method, process, activity, incentive, or reward that is believed to be more effective at delivering a particular outcome than any other technique, method, process, etc., when applied to a particular condition or circumstance. According to other definitions, best practices describe the most efficient (least amount of effort) and effective (best results) way of accomplishing a task, based on repeatable procedures that have proven themselves over time for large numbers of people.

In IT, best practices has many meanings. Sometimes best practices consist of templates that come with a software package. These templates contain certain workflows, business processes, standard reports and performance indicators. Step-by-step manuals on how to best implement the software or "hints and tips" (e.g., how to best tune a database or parameterize an application) are also considered by some to be best practices.

The idea of best practices is very attractive. "Plug and play" and "plain vanilla" are terms often heard when best practices are advocated. Adopting them minimizes the risk in a project. After all, the essence of best practices is that they are proven, so you can't go wrong. Because best practices are bound to be more complete than what you could have come up with yourself, you don't have to reinvent the wheel. You can stand on the shoulders of others. What could be wrong about learning from others, while at the same time saving heaps of time and money?

And learning from best practices shouldn't be limited to your specific industry; other industries may have already solved the problems you are facing.

Another great thing about best practices is that they can form the basis of a benchmark[1]. Benchmarking is used to measure the performance of a certain activity and compare it to a peer group within the company, or a peer group of other companies. If you share the same set of processes, way of working, or means of data collection, there is a common basis to compare. This comparison informs you how much better you are than average-in-class or how far removed you are from best-in-class. The measure of success can be anything, ranging from operational measures such as cost, quality and speed, to more strategic measures such as vision, agility, or alignment.

Best practices are not without criticism. The objection most heard is that although a best practice may work in one situation, it may not work when you change the context or the circumstances. For instance, a best practice top-down software implementation may not work in an organization that has a culture that favors bottom-up solutions. Different organizations have different maturity levels, skills and capabilities. Someone else's best practices could be your worst nightmare. The context of the best practice should be known before you try to apply it. How much of an issue this can be depends on the type of best practice being considered... When considering technical best practices, such as ways to tune a database, it is easier to recognize, change or create the right circumstances. This is harder to achieve when dealing with management best practices, such as a certain decision-making process

---

1 It is not clear where the term benchmark comes from. Some say it originates from the chiseled horizontal marks made in stone structures, into which an angle iron could be placed to form a "bench" for a leveling rod. Another theory is that the term benchmarking was first used by cobblers to measure people's feet for shoes. They would place someone's foot on a "bench" and mark it out to make the pattern for the shoes.

or a change management approach. However, there are other objections that are more fundamental of nature.

Competing Schools of Thought

The problem with best practices is that there are so many of them, and often they conflict with each other. Each discipline has rigorously thought through its approach and has written the "bible" on the subject, usually including a comprehensive overview of do's and don'ts. In various disciplines, arguments about which approach is correct can go on for tens of years. Remember knowledge management from the 1990s? There were two schools of thought. One school presented the view that knowledge is tacit and located within an individual and his unique frame of reference. Therefore, knowledge management should focus on expertise location, helping people find other people who have certain knowledge.

The other school of thought was convinced that knowledge is explicit and can be extracted, codified and stored in systems. Users could access these systems for specific knowledge or these systems could actively support users in their work. Although the term knowledge management is not used that much anymore, the ideology – and discussion for that matter – is back with a vengeance. Enterprise 2.0, consisting of all kinds of collaboration technologies, and Semantic Web, codifying the meaning of information, are bound to keep the discussion alive for many years to come. Similar discussions have taken place in for instance data warehousing, business process management and probably most other fields in IT and business as well.

Multiple issues unravel if you start thinking about this. While discussions continue for many years, technology itself is moving on. While complete groups of professionals are debating between right and wrong, the actual problem that needs to be solved is forgotten. Often a best practice is based on dealing with certain limitations or constraints. These can be cost, time, performance, capacity or anything else of a technical nature. In short, best practices are the solutions for yesterday's problems.

Furthermore, when there are multiple, even conflicting, best practices that are preached, how can you determine which one is really the best? For every success story, there is a success story for the opposite approach as well. And for every success story that you hear, there is a story in which the best practice completely failed. The only logical conclusion is that the success of a best practice is not in the best practice itself, but in the fact that you simply pick one way of doing things, and make sure everyone does it the same way. Creating alignment itself may be more important than how things are done. You could say that a best practice is a best practice *because* it is a best practice.

In itself there is nothing wrong with this practice. The result is the same: a successful initiative. It doesn't matter if the success comes through the specifics of the approach or because people simply used a single approach. In fact, a whole school of philosophers, the consequentialists, have argued the same. Although the consequentialists looked at it from a moral point of view – the consequences of an action determine whether the action was morally right or wrong – I am sure they would agree. They might not have literally said, "Hey, if it works, it works," when it comes to best practices, but it is the same principle.

But I don't buy it, I must admit. I find it too easy. Using a best practice for the sake of the best practice, even if it works, skips an important step: actually understanding what you are doing. If you are looking for a quick solution, best practices don't invite you to think for yourself. There is a risk they achieve the opposite by inviting you to blindly copy what others have done. That's not going to give you a better understanding of your business. In fact, when a best practice is deployed –particularly if you belong to a certain school of thought – it is probably because that is the way you were taught. And that is simply called "dogma."

Dogma versus Reason

If best practices are not questioned, they become dogma.

Dogma is Greek for "that which seems to one, opinion or belief" and is derived from the Greek term *dokeo*, "to think, to suppose, to imagine." A more neutral term for it then would be *doctrine*, which comes from Latin and means "that which is taught." Dogma is an established belief held by a religion, ideology or group of people that is considered to be absolutely true, regardless of evidence or lack of evidence to support it, and is not to be disputed. Although dogma exists in all ages, it was dominant in the Middle Ages. Questioning how the world worked was asking for trouble.

Ask Galileo Galilei (1564-1642). Galileo questioned the then-current idea of geocentrism, the idea that the earth is the center of the universe and that all other objects circle around it. He advocated heliocentrism, placing the sun at the center of the universe. Galileo was forced by the Inquisition to take it back and apologize, as the idea was "false and contrary to Scripture" (dogma!), and at age 69 was sentenced to house arrest for the rest of his life. Today we would call Galileo's courage to challenge dogma a *career-limiting move*. Indeed, dogma can be found in modern organizations as well. In many companies, there are questions that you simply don't ask, and beliefs you simply don't question.

Dogma was considered unacceptable by the philosophers that emerged in the Age of Enlightenment. The Age of Enlightenment is the name of the political and philosophical movement that started in France, England, Scotland and Germany. This period, roughly between 1650 and the end of the 18th century (the French Revolution), completely transformed the world view on culture, science, religion and politics within the Western world. The term *Enlightenment* contrasts the new era to the old Dark Ages, and is a reaction on Middle Ages that were ruled by dogma and belief in authority. In fact, the authors of the American Declaration of Independence were highly influenced by Enlightenment principles ("Life, Liberty and the pursuit of Happiness").

The basis of the Age of Reason and Enlightenment is the idea that we should be guided by rationality and reason, instead of faith. Science over religion. Philosophers such as Spinoza, Voltaire, Locke, Hobbes, Smith and Kant sought ways to change society by freeing the people from the restraints of tradition and feudal authority. A few Enlightenment principles shine a surprisingly relevant light on best practices.

Think for Yourself

It is pretty clear how German philosopher Immanuel Kant (1724-1804) would have looked at best practices. In fact, his view can be found in his very definition of Enlightenment: "Enlightenment is man's emergence from his self-imposed immaturity. Immaturity is the inability to use one's understanding without guidance from another. This immaturity is self-imposed when its cause lies not in lack of understanding, but in lack of resolve and courage to use it without guidance from another." In his essay "What is Enlightenment?" (1784), he continues to explain what he means: "Laziness and cowardice are the reasons why so great a proportion of men (...) nonetheless gladly remain in lifelong immaturity, and why it is so easy for others to establish themselves as their guardians. It is so easy to be immature. If I have a book to serve as my understanding, a pastor to serve as my conscience, a physician to determine my diet for me, and so on, I need not exert myself at all."

Exerting yourself by making the effort to think seems to imply that Kant felt the process of coming to a solution itself had value, that it would lead to enlightenment and truly understanding what you are talking about. This thought is not new; in fact, the old Greek philosopher Socrates did nothing else but challenge assumptions by questioning them. Of course, this was seen as extremely dangerous by the Greek authorities and he was sentenced to death. It seems that in our Western management culture, we have adopted that sense of danger again. It is better to stick to what we know, and copy what someone else has done, to limit our risk exposure. Laziness and cowardice, indeed? Fortunately, independent thinkers in management are not sentenced to death anymore, but often they are ignored.

Belief in Technological Advancements

In the Age of Enlightenment, science was developing with enormous speed. Sir Isaac Newton (1642-1727) formulated the law of gravity, invented calculus, and worked out the constituents of light. He, and others, believed that the universe was based on rules only waiting to be discovered. The Enlightenment philosophers believed this to be true for all areas of science, including the social sciences. Francis Bacon (1561-1626) was one of the first to see that advancements in understanding the rules of reality would lead to having greater control over reality, and more possibilities to change and improve society at large.

These philosophers would probably agree that best practices are solutions to yesterday's problems. They would have argued that the future had more to offer than the past. The future holds infinite possibilities that only have to be discovered. They probably would have liked what current management guru C.K. Prahalad wrote about *next practices* just before he passed away in 2010. Prahalad argues that best practices may help enterprises catch up with competitors, but it won't turn them into market leaders. Organizations become winners by spotting big opportunities and inventing next practices. In Prahalad's words: "Next practices are all about innovation: imagining what the future will look like, identifying the mega-opportunities that will arise, and building capabilities to capitalize on them." In the true spirit of Enlightenment, Prahalad also says that "If you look for ways to develop next practices, opportunities abound. In fact, executives are constrained not by resources but by their imagination." He then quotes Peter Drucker, who once said that the best opportunities are "visible, but not seen." They're just waiting to be uncovered. According to the Enlightenment philosophers, best practices are the solutions for yesterday's problems indeed.

No Single Truth

Although the Age of Enlightenment was a collective reaction on the Dark Ages, it didn't mean all philosophers agreed. In fact, in search for reason and in discovering a new view on the world, many philosophies were conflicting, flat-out contradiciting each other and highly divergent. The Enlightenment was less a set of ideas than it was a set of values.

The same is the case when examining best practices. There are multiple schools of thought, often competing with each other, and sometimes even completely ignoring each other. Science has taught us about "theory." A theory is the best possible explanation for a certain phenomenon, until a better explanation emerges. At the minimum, best practices should be interpreted the same way. It is great to have found a way that works for you, but as circumstances change, it is important to remain rational and keep questioning what you believe in. Perhaps there is something to be said about other schools of thought as well. Perhaps there are new, emerging ways of doing things that require open investigation – not with the old best practice in mind, but on their own merits.

Georg Wilhelm Friedrich Hegel (1770-1831) described his ideas a bit later than the Age of Enlightenment. In his description of the history of philosophy, he formulated a powerful concept that later became known as thesis-antithesis-synthesis. A thesis is a situation, a state of being, a paradigm that we believe to be true, like a best practice. This is followed by a reaction – like the Age of Enlightenment – usually arguing the opposite and pointing out the fallacies of the thesis. This is called the antithesis. Over time these contradictory positions reconcile, and a higher truth or a middle ground is found. This is called the synthesis. As one of those ironies in life, the synthesis becomes the new thesis, with all its advantages and disadvantages, inevitably followed by a new antithesis, and so on.

Competing schools of thought in philosophy, or in any other discipline for that matter, are a good thing – at least if you agree with Hegel. People who subscribe to a best practice should not dig trenches and dismiss other schools of thought, but should actively embrace them. Through examination of what they have in common, and by seeking to reconcile their differences, you come closer to a synthesis, creating a "better best practice"[2].

Why Now?

There are many parallels between the past and the present. The Age of Enlightenment coincided with a growing economy, growing population and a growing middle class. Urbanization increased, and the first signs of what we now call consumerism appeared. Furthermore, in the West we learned more about Eastern cultures and the great civilizations of non-Christian cultures. And perhaps most importantly, science was developing with enormous speed. Many constraints were lifted, and it was simply time to question the old ways and reinvent society. Dogma was for the poor, the illiterate and the ignorant. Enlightenment was a step up in Maslow's hierarchy of human needs, from being concerned about physiological needs, safety, and a sense of belonging to being concerned about esteem and self-actualization.

Current themes in IT greatly resemble the circumstances of the Age of Enlightenment. Back then science was developing at an incredible rate; today, technology is. We are now almost completely globalized and get real-time information from all over the world[3]. The current generation (Generation Y) grew up using information technology, they are the growing middle class of information. Many of the constraints we were working under have been lifted. Hardware capacity is growing, and bandwidth and connectivity through the Internet seem unlimited in the modern world. The Information Age of Enlightenment redefines how we think, live and work. In the dramatic words of Jean-Paul Sartre (1905-1980): "We

---

2 It is clear by now that the term best practice itself is problematic because it supposes a practice cannot be improved. Proponents will argue that best practices are simply succeeded by new best practices, and that best practices are best at the time
3 This may be true for large parts of our economy, and for Internet technology, but definitely not for politics and society.

are free to reinvent ourselves. If we see ourselves as only objects with fixed identities, we cease to Be."

Self-Defeating Prophecy

Although I've spent more words criticizing best practices than validating them, it seems both arguments are equally convincing. Best practices lead to average results and you should think for yourself versus it is better to stand on the shoulders of giants and learn from what others have done. In short, should best practices be adopted, adapted or abandoned?

The best practice for using best practices (this would be a meta best practice) is to admit that best practices per definition are a self-defeating prophecy. If everyone adopts them, who's the best? At the very least, best practices should be called something else. For non-competitive areas, copying what others are doing is a very good idea. You know you'll be fine and that's enough. In fact, in those areas it would even be conceivable to adapt the organization to the best practice instead of the other way around. The goal would be simply to achieve regulatory compliance, to create a benchmark based on reasonable cost, or to not have to bother too much so that the company's leaders can focus on more competitive areas. We should not refer to best practices in this case, but to "shared practices."

Most strategists agree that a successful strategy differentiates your organization from the competition. Therefore, in those areas that are most competitive, another approach to best practices is needed. In those areas, best practices per definition cannot be "best," because they need to be different. Best practices in these situations should be referred to as "baseline practices." Based on a sound understanding what others have learned, these practices are only the starting point. They need to be heavily adapted to the unique requirements and capabilities of the organization. And you know what, perhaps the best thing you can learn from a best practice is to reverse it and do the exact opposite.

Technology, What Have You Done for Me Lately?

*Any sufficient advanced technology
is indistinguishable from magic.*
- Arthur C. Clarke

The moment marketing took control over the term "paradigm shift," it basically lost its meaning. "Our new version of the software, 11.7, marks a complete paradigm shift compared to 11.6." What would the step from version 12 to version 13 be then? Moving into a new, parallel universe?

The word paradigm, not surprisingly, is Greek. It is based on the terms *paradeigma*, which means a pattern or example; *paradeiknumi*, which means to represent or to expose; and the combination of *para* (beside, by) and *deiknumi* (to point out). In normal terms, a paradigm is a general agreement and belief of how the world works. This goes deeper than simply subscribing to a certain theory of something. A paradigm represents our foundational point of view. In fact, the desire to experience the world through the development of theories is actually a paradigm in itself. And there could be other paradigms to experience the world, for instance by trying to simply sense it.

A paradigm shift, a term used by American physicist and philosopher Thomas Kuhn (1922-1996), is what happens when the general agreement on how the world works fundamentally changes. We have seen this a number of times in the world of philosophy. The end of the Greek dominance in philosophy was the beginning of the Dark Ages in Europe. It was change in paradigm, where philosophy became dominated by religion. In turn, the Age of Enlightenment marked a turn in which philosophy became dominated by science.

Although the term *paradigm shift* may be overused in technology, it is hard to deny that the IT industry is characterized by a high turnover of paradigms; they seem to be shifting all the time. Think, for instance, of computing paradigms. Computing started as a highly centralized activity involving mainframes and data centers. The advent of the personal computer marked a shift to decentralized computing (or, indeed, personal computing) and – in corporate environments – client/server architectures. The Internet pushed a complete new paradigm, back to a more centralized approach, lately involving "the cloud." And now, just when even the greatest critics and laggards bought into the Internet and "zero footprint" as the end-game of computing paradigms, we enter the Era of App.

In the end, as much impact as they have, the fast-changing paradigms are relatively superficial. They are delivery mechanisms, or simply directions for optimization. There is a much deeper, underlying and more interesting paradigm shift going on. Much deeper and underlying, because it affects much more than just computing styles and more interesting because it is taking place now. The paradigm shift that is taking place is changing what technology means for us.

What is Technology?

Defining technology seems very simple at first glance. Technology involves all things or artifacts that help us to perform a task, better than with our bare hands or bodies. This includes a spearhead or a match, as well as a photo camera or an iPad. Some technology artifacts would be called low-tech, such as the wheel or an axe. Others would be considered high-tech, such as solar-energy pads or pacemakers.

But, as with so many philosophical exercises, once we start thinking it through, it becomes messy. The problem with this definition is that the more you consider it, the more things have to be called technology. Intuitively, I wouldn't consider a newspaper technology, but it helps a journalist report the news, which helps readers keep up with what is happening in the world and form opinions on it.

Let's explore a more precise definition. The word *technology* comes from the Greek terms *techne*, which means "skill or craft," and *logia*, which translates to "the study of." So technology means something intangible, the study of a skill or craft. This study then leads to a body of knowledge regarding a certain craft, say woodwork, or digitally capturing video. This body of knowledge may be applied to produce something, such as a chair or a video camera. These are not technologies themselves (obvious in the case of a chair, confusing when considering a video camera), but simply devices containing that body of knowledge. So, in this view, a smartphone is not a technology, but the result of applying many different technologies.

This definition is problematic in exactly the same way as the first definition – the scope becomes impractically big. For instance, this definition can also be used to refer to "democracy" or "socialism." Both are the result of the implementation of a body of knowledge; in this case, the skill of organizing a society. And indeed, some do refer to forms of governance as social technology.

So, it is hard to limit the definition of technology. And there is continuous confusion between the colloquial use of the term technology, referring to devices, and the formal definition, which is intangible in nature. I will call the first definition *concrete*, as in this view technology requires a physical shape; it becomes a piece of technology. The second definition is *abstract* in nature, as a body of knowledge can be under continuous development; it is what enables to build the instance of technology, e.g., a device.

I will use the more practical definition of technology here. Although it is less precise, it helps create an easier understanding of where technology is going and what that means for us.

What Does Technology Mean?

Technology has known various paradigms over thousands of years. Up to the 18th century, we have seen the craftsman's paradigm of technology. Knowledge was passed from father to son. Technological devices were built by the craftsman himself, or came from specialists close by. A craftsman had a very good understanding of how the technological artifacts worked, and was an expert user of them. There was no industrialization; most likely, technological devices varied in how they were created, what they looked like, and also how they were used. In today's terms, we would say this technology paradigm offers personal productivity.

With the advent of the Industrial Age, the technology paradigm changed. Technology didn't mean personal productivity anymore, but was aimed at completely automating tasks, rendering humans unnecessary in many cases. Technology become much more centralized, and aimed to achieve economies of scale. We entered the engineering paradigm into technology. This paradigm shift did not take place without resistance, as per usual in any revolution. Ned Ludd[1] was most famous for his resistance. In 1779, Ludd, an English weaver, supposedly smashed two knitting frames. Somehow the story spread, and whenever there was a case of sabotage of knitting frames, Ludd (jokingly) was blamed for it. Although there is no proof that Ludd smashed the frames because he was opposing this new technology, by 1812 he became the figurehead of professional frame breakers, later also known as Luddites.

Now, in the 21st century, we are amidst the next technology paradigm. The Internet has had infinitely more impact on our daily lives than even the wildest predictions imagined at the end of the 1990s. Critics were fast to dismiss everything 2.0 as hype, but it has transformed the way we work and how we communicate (and Web 3.0, that adds semantic technology to the mix, is well under way). In fact, as the first members of what is called Generation Y, also known as the millennials or the Net Generation, are entering the workforce, management practices are changing and so are the technologies used in the workplace. It is not uncommon that business users know more about modern IT than IT professionals, and it is fairly common that business users bring their own devices from home, and demand to be able to use them in the workplace.

---

1 His true existence was actually never confirmed

Again, the meaning of technology has changed. Technology now is supposed to augment human capability and not just on the personal level. It is supposed to connect humanity and human capabilities on a global level as well. We believe that technology does not have any meaning in itself, unlike the engineering view, and that technological thinking is our evolutionary advantage. Technology and devices help us compensate for all the things we don't have or can't do. Humans cannot fly, are not strong, are not very fast, can't handle extreme heat or cold and cannot swim very well. Technology gives us all the capabilities we do not possess ourselves.

There is a distinct dynamic taking place in how the meaning of technology has been evolving, one that has been described before in philosophy, by Georg Wilhelm Friedrich Hegel (1770-1831). The dynamic is known as the Hegelian dialectic. Hegel's dialectic consists of a three-step process: thesis-antithesis-synthesis.[2] The process starts with a current situation or common wisdom, called the *thesis*. The situation usually has a strong disadvantage, such as an unexplainable phenomenon in a theory, or needs of people not being met. This leads to people adopting the opposite belief, approach or situation. This reaction is called the *antithesis*. It solves the previous disadvantage, but brings new disadvantages as well. (In fact, both thesis and antithesis present dominant disadvantages.) Hegel then introduces the idea of *synthesis*, where over time the two opposites will fuse, or reconcile, creating the best of both worlds. And then, interestingly enough, the synthesis becomes the new thesis – what is believed to be true – to be eventually challenged by an antithesis once again. The pendulum swings, but on a higher plane.

The similarities between the Hegelian dialectic and

---

2 Although this model is often named after Hegel, he himself never used that specific formulation. Hegel ascribed that terminology to Immanuel Kant. Carrying on Kant's work, Johann Gottlieb Fichte greatly elaborated on the synthesis model and popularized it.

the development of the meaning of technology are striking. The craftsman's view represents the thesis, a situation that had been accepted for thousands of years. However, technology did not scale. This was completely fixed by the antithesis of the industrial revolution, but it led to the opposite problem – technology didn't help people but subjected them. Today's view on technology represents the synthesis between the two, giving people the power to create global productivity for everyone's benefit.[3]

Augmenting Human Capabilities

Understanding to which technology paradigm you subscribe, and understanding to which paradigm the people you work with subscribe, helps avoid a lot of pointless discussion. People representing different paradigms will never be able to agree what a "good" system is, as "good" is usually defined as to which extent the object of choice is reaching its goals. No common understanding of goals leads to no common understanding of what is good. From a business perspective, understanding the technology paradigm of your software vendors will also help predict the success of your products. More than examining features and functions, understanding the underlying paradigm tells you if there is a vision match that is needed for long-term success. Table 1 will help you understand various aspects of the technology paradigms we have seen so far. I will abstain from the craftsman's view (as it is less relevant today), and compare the engineering and humanistic approach.

Generally, in the engineering paradigm we take an *analytical* view. We look at all the components of a problem, and see how they work or should work. We then determine the best way they work, and automate that process. Then, this newly automated best practice can be copied and repeated. The success of such an approach is in hav-

---

3 This is not reality in every aspect yet, but it seems to be a widely accepted vision.

	Engineering	Humanistic
Problem solving	Identify best practice, automate and replicate	Technology enables all users to create their individual best solution, and share those views
Functionality	Value the functions and features	Value capabilities to flexibly meet changing user requirements, and interacting with other systems
Transparency	You should be able to understand how the system works	IT should be ubiquitous and you shouldn't even see it
Software management	Complete control over software	Open source, allowing everyone to contribute
Programming style	Prescriptive (describe all details)	Declarative (describe boundaries)
User experience	Lots of options everywhere	Just showing relevant options
Training	Train users how to use the system	Train the system how to support the users

Table 1: Characteristics of the engineering and humanistic paradigm

ing a clear set of boundary conditions; in other words, a clear scope of the system or concept we are examining. Within those boundaries, we can optimize and find ways to offer the best breadth and depth of functionality.

The humanistic paradigm takes a more *synthetic* view. We look at how the different components can interact with each other. This is a bigger worry than determining whether the components have exhaustive functionality. After all, the evolving use of a system cannot be predicted anyway. It is better keep all options open, and ensure that a system is open enough to plug in new functional requirements later. This way, the concept of the system is bigger than the sum of the components. Together they form a certain idea. The system is not optimized towards one way of working, but optimized to cater to every user with a specific way of working, depending on the user's own wishes or the specifics of the case at hand.

Technologies, or technology providers, can operate in multiple paradigms at the same time. Look at Apple, for instance. People simply and intuitively "work" with an iPod; there is no manual needed. Children know how to operate an iPhone or an iPad before the age of two. Design and technology cannot be separated from each other; they are inextricably linked within the concept. At the same time, Apple likes to keep complete control over the technology, to ensure a consistent user experience. To achieve that, Apple covers the complete stack from hardware and operating system to approving applications and managing the distribution of software though iTunes. For the iPad, Apple even goes as far to exclude standard technologies such as Adobe Flash, because Flash could be used to create alternative user interfaces. Apple is at the forefront of the humanistic paradigm, and at the same time among the most conservative of technology providers.

The Next Technology Paradigm

Technology development is not an entirely autonomous process. There are definitely evolutionary aspects to innovation, and countless inventions and technologies that never really saw the light of day. It is clear that technology has a profound – perhaps even defining – impact on society, but society affects technology development as well. Without the Age of Enlightenment there would not have been such attention to science, and it would have been harder for scientists to fund their research. Also, scientists and engineers are a product of their time as well, because their work is inspired by their environment, whether the inspiration is based on needs or the desire to change something. The innovation effect is then further magnified because many technology innovations build on top of each other. Throughout history, technology has had different meanings, based on the needs of society. Up to the Industrial Age, technology helped people survive in nature. Technology in the Industrial Age helped people not only to conquer nature, but to produce more complex goods. Society detached itself from nature, and technology became more conceptual; hence, the lack of focus on human beings. Now, developments in society revolve around freedom and democracy (to which extent these two terms are complementary or contradictory I leave to the reader), and again so does technology.

No one can predict the future. The best we can do is be ready for whatever the future brings. We can craft a number of scenarios, in which we imagine different futures. Not for the sake of being right, but in order to be ready for whatever happens. Having scenarios in which we describe various options trains us to keep our eyes open for any indications the current paradigm isn't working anymore. Imagining potential future scenarios also helps you develop a critical eye towards the current situation and not take it for granted.

If we understand the underlying dynamic to paradigm shifts in IT, following Hegel's dialectic, we might be able to imagine some pretty unthinkable things, even in the short term.

If the humanistic approach is the synthesis between an engineering approach and the craftsman's approach, according to dialectical logic it becomes the new thesis, the "new normal," if you will. Again, according to dialectical logic, this will invariably lead to a new antithesis. What will that antithesis look like? Many predictions are possible.

One particularly interesting prediction for the world of IT, following dialectical logic, is actually that not much will happen in the years to come. If we look at the myriad of corporate IT systems and the amount of application overhaul that needs to take place to truly innovate, in combination with shrinking IT budgets, it will not be easy to adopt new technologies. This scenario might be called "grinding halt," fed by the antithesis of "no change." If you consider that the thesis in IT has always been continuous change, the opposite might happen as well. Although this might not come true at all, it helps us open our eyes in regard to the current situation. Can we sustain our current IT landscapes? Are they agile enough to absorb new technologies? Will our legacy not hold us back too much?

Another possible antithesis comes from considering Metcalfe's law. It states that the value of a telecommunications network is proportional to the square of the number of the connected users. The same principle applies seamlessly to social networks, and because of the influence of social networks on the way people like to communicate and share information, on information management in general. In short, the more users there are for certain relevant pieces of information, the more it is worth. This fits the humanistic paradigm perfectly.

As an antithesis to this, we could reverse Metcalfe's law, which actually is how the economy usually works: the higher the scarcity of a good, the higher the value. Today, the value of IT is expressed in terms of maximization of distribution; the next paradigm could be about IT exclusivity. Only the privileged may get access to certain information, and communities may change from being open and inclusive to being "by invitation and nomination only." Again, this idea may never become a reality, but it is good to be ready for it, or – when possible – to fight this possible next reality. Although IT exclusivity may be an unlikely scenario at first, it could very well be the result of a few other trends that are to be witnessed in business. Think, for instance, of economic protectionism, polarizing politics, and stifling regulatory issues.

However, like the delivery paradigms of mainframe computing, client/server and internet computing, these are all short-term developments. The next big paradigm promises to go full circle. So far we have treated technology as an exogenous factor, where artifacts helped us augment our capabilities. The different things we have expected technology to do for us were aligned with the paradigms in society, from survival to freedom.

The first signs towards an entirely new technological paradigm are visible already, specifically in biotechnology. Today this term is mostly reserved for using living organisms and bioprocesses in technology, but increasingly, this may also become the other way around: introducing technology within the human body to strengthen human capabilities – endogenous technology.

Using the paradigm shifts from exogenous technology, following Maslow's hierarchy of needs, we can even predict the path endogenous technologies may take. The first breakthroughs for endogenous technologies are visible already, helping people with their health. Strictly speaking, an adjustable gastric band is already endogenous technology. A pacemaker might communicate with a monitoring service to give early warnings about pending heart failures. Nanotechnologies may circulate in the blood or earphones may be replaced with electronic hearing membranes.

The next step might be in creating more personal safety and esteem by creating "super powers." Perhaps we will find technological ways to increase the power of our muscles, so we can lift more or run faster. The first field is most likely to be the military, but my bet for the second area for technological development like this to be successful would be in sports.

Then there would be a next round of what we now call information technology built into our brains. It will help us remember more, perhaps "plug in" additional knowledge through a modern version of a USB port, or take augmented reality to an entirely new level. Today augmented reality means plotting information on top of a picture on our smartphone, tablet, or even eyeglasses. The endogenous version might do the same, but by placing information directly on the retina or even the visual cortex. This is when we are near what Ray Kurzweil calls the "singularity": the confluence of man and machine.

Can Computers Think?

Artificial life form and Lt. Commander Data on Star Trek The Next Generation:
"My circuitry will need to adapt. It will take some time before they can compensate for your input."

Translation: "Geordi, I will miss you."

I am having trouble writing this essay. Somehow my computer has a mind of its own today. He is a bit slow and isn't really very responsive. I don't know what's wrong with him today. Maybe tomorrow he'll feel like himself again.

Have you ever caught yourself attributing human characteristics to your computer or to your car? (Lots of people, including myself, even give their car a name and can describe its personality.) You most likely do so to your cat, dog or even your goldfish. We all do this, and it is perfectly normal. We pat our computers on the back, we tell customers on the phone that "he doesn't want to" today, or – in the spur of a techno-anger moment – we even hit our computers. YouTube is full of funny videos of people doing all this. Does it help? Does the computer behave better? What would happen if you would ignore your computer for a week after he (it) let you down? Or even better, could you make your Windows-based computer jealous by threatening to move to Apple? Nothing would happen, of course. We know that.

Turing Test

Still, it seems to be deeply human to describe things around us in our own – human – terms. Perhaps this is also the reason why the question "Can computers think?" is such a popular one in modern philosophy. The most influential person who has reflected on this question is undoubtedly Alan Turing (1912-1954). Turing was a pioneer in computer science and was responsible for cracking the German Enigma encryption machine during World War II. In a 1950 paper that is a remarkably good read, "Computing Machinery and Intelligence," Turing introduced what is now known as the Turing test. Turing replaces the question of whether computers can think with a more practical one: Is it imaginable that a computer could fool a human being, and be taken for a human being as well?

The test that Turing devised described – and I am summarizing here – a situation in which a test person could ask a question to both another human being and a computer, without being able to see who was who. They would communicate through a computer screen. The test person would be allowed to ask questions, and the other human being and the computer would give answers. Both the other human being and the computer would even be allowed to cheat and respond with statements such as, "Don't listen to him. I am the real human being." To emulate the slower human speed, the computer would also be allowed to wait before responding to mathematical questions, for instance. If the test person could not to distinguish the difference, the computer passed the Turing test and would seemingly be able to think – in other words, display intelligence.

The Turing test provides a very practical solution to a very hard philosophical problem. What is intelligence anyway, and what does it mean to think? But the Turing test has been widely criticized, too. Because of its practical solution, it equates intelligent behavior with human behavior. This is not necessarily the case. Humans can display extremely unintelligent behavior (like hitting their computer and thinking it helps). And who says that human intelligence or the human way of thinking is the only way of thinking? People, and their cognitive capabilities, cannot be separated from their bodies and their senses. Why would computers have to be limited to means of communication such as language?

Maybe the concept of thinking can be defined in completely non-human ways. Ironically, if computers perform at their best thinking capacity in non-human ways (and you can argue computers do this all the time already), they would completely fail the Turing test instead of acing all intelligence tests.

Turing wrote his paper in 1950, so what he describes was pretty far-out thinking for his day. Nevertheless, he was very concrete in his predictions. He expected that by the year 2000, computers would pass the Turing test at about 70%. In his view, storage was the bottleneck, and he expected it to be "10^9" by 2000. Assuming he was counting in bytes, this would be 10 gigabytes. It seems reality did overtake this prediction considerably! But what about the prediction of getting it right by 70%?

IBM, Chess and Jeopardy!

Turing ends his paper with a small discussion on where to start emulating human intelligence. Turing suggests an abstract activity first, such as playing chess; and in, fact, this is exactly what happened. IBM's computer, Deep Blue, did defeat chess champion Garry Kasparov. The programming of Deep Blue was largely one of brute force, calculating an unbelievable 200 million positions per second and "thinking through" six to eight moves in advance. Additionally, Deep Blue contained a huge library of 700,000 chess games. The developments didn't stop with Deep Blue's victory. Today's chess software running on standard PCs may not calculate as many moves per second, but contain much smarter algorithms.

Moreover, IBM has successfully moved beyond chess and has succeeded in a much, much harder domain. In 2011, the IBM Watson computer won the American game show *Jeopardy!*, beating the two best contestants the show ever had. At the core of Watson was an engine to parse language, including trying to understand clever word play and slang, on which many of the show's questions hinge. The computer's programming was a combination of many different styles of algorithms trying to interpret the questions, in combination with four terabytes of semantically structured information – an infinitely more complex task than playing chess. Still, Watson is far from passing the Turing test. It may interpret language better than any other computer, but it is focused on providing answers instead of full conversation.

Returning to the original question, what does it mean for a computer to think, or to display intelligence? To even define what thinking really means is challenging already. Taking a very rational approach, thinking comes very close to reasoning and problem solving, where thinking describes the process of going through the various steps. Consequently, the more complex the problems you can solve, the more intelligent you are. According to the IQ tests, at least. Using this definition, it is hard to deny that computers can think; in fact, they think much better than human beings do. Take, for instance, the "logic grid"[1] puzzles that have been so popular for a while. For instance, based on a list of logical clues, one fills in a grid that shows the ages, hobbies and favorite colors of Casper, Rosaly, Emilie and Wilhelmine.

	Casper	Rosaly	Emilie	Wilhelmine	Pink	Orange	Green	Black
2010								
2007								
1996								
1999								
Playground								
Playing drums								
Gymnastics								
Hip hop dancing								

Figure 1: Logic grid puzzle

As this is a fairly simple algorithm, computers crack these puzzles in a millisecond. Moreover, they can do it on a much more abstract level than we can. Where we need real-world clues, like phone numbers, names and hobbies to

---

1 http://www.logic-puzzles.org/

imagine the logic, computers just need a label, and Rosaly as a label does just as fine as C2.

The What and How of Thinking

Others define thinking as a much more organic process, full of lateral steps, and also include thinking in terms of images, emotions, and so forth. When thinking includes imagination and inventive approaches to problems, this is where we human beings excel. I remember hearing a story that the American military was using pattern recognition software for visual processing. In particular, it was trying to create software that would recognize tanks, to avoid shooting at the wrong ones. The software was fed as many pictures as possible about American tanks, as well as other tanks, and through learning algorithms the software got better and better at recognizing them, until the software had to perform its capabilities based on live feeds instead of pictures. The software engineers later found out what had gone wrong. Instead of recognizing the patterns of the actual tanks in the pictures, the software started to recognize the resolution of the pictures. Pictures of American tanks had higher resolution than the pictures of foreign ones.

Thus it seems there are two ways to think about thinking: the "what" way and the "how" way. Turing chooses the "what" way; he only focuses on the outcome, an intelligent result. If we follow this way of thinking, we cannot escape the conclusion that computers can think. In fact, they can think much better than we can. They can reason better, faster and deeper than human beings, with much more precision. Getting to the same broad level of thinking than humans can is simply a matter of time. Support for this thought comes from the analytical philosophers, a twentieth century school of thought led by Bertrand Russell (1872-1970) and Ludwig Wittgenstein (1889-1951). In their view, people can only think what they have words for. If there is no word for it, it cannot be thought. (Even if this is not true, the moment something new is thought, in order to express it, it needs a word.) In essence, although we are not that far yet, you can codify all thought; and if it can be codified, it can be fed to a computer.

The "how" way presents a very surprising view. It seems there is a stronger tendency in research to explain human thinking in terms of computer science than the other way around. Many scientists and philosophers currently describe the world as consisting of matter only, subjected to the laws of nature. Applied to the human brain, according to some (not all) neurologists and psychologists, this means it is nothing more than an incredibly complex neurocomputer. Human behavior is simply the result of neuro stimuli. In fact, as the brain doesn't have a central command center, but consists of many different pieces interacting with each other, one currently popular belief is that it the brain doesn't even make most decisions. The body has decided already it wants to eat the lovely smelling food even before the brain has interpreted the scent. The body already reacts by withdrawing the hand from a hot surface fractions of a second before the information reaches the brain. Recent research shows that, in some cases, the brain gets involved only slightly *after* the body gears towards action. As some put it in extreme terms, for a large part of our daily behavior, the brain is a "chatterbox" that rationalizes behavior and actions after the fact.

Seen this way, there is no reason to suggest that computers cannot think. Decision making is a distributed mechanism involving many centers in the brain. Thinking would be comparable to an internal dialogue. Computers would again be better at it than human beings. In fact, this is exactly how the IBM Watson computer was programmed, with multiple algorithms for grammatical analysis, information retrieval, information comparison, and formulating answers. Even better than a human being, a computer could contain algorithms (bots) following different paradigms (whereas most human beings have trouble handling multiple, or even conflicting, paradigms at the same time). Such a distributed and diverse process could lead to much more balanced outcomes (or a much more serious version of schizophrenia, now that I come to think of it).

In many ways, defining the brain as a large and complex neurocomputer represents a full circle from the Age of Enlightenment, which was at its height in the 18th century[2]. Philosophers aired an unshakable belief in the power of science. The world and the universe were seen as a machine – an incredibly complicated one, but a machine nevertheless. Our job, then, is simply to figure out the rules, as is the same with the brain today. It is an incredibly complicated neurocomputer, and it is up to us to figure out how it works.

Judgment Day

In one way or another, computers can think, but somehow the conclusion doesn't really satisfy me. It somehow *feels* wrong that our human thinking can be reduced to pure reasoning.

I am more than happy to accept that computers can reason much better than we can, and infinitely faster. But there is a clue in the "logic grid" puzzles I described. Computers can do this in pure mathematical form, while human beings benefit from labels such as names and hobbies. Labels make us *understand* what we are thinking about. Do computers have that understanding too? When a person understands something, its meaning is clear to him or her.

When is a meaning clear? Perhaps things, ideas or concepts can have inherent meaning, worth and significance in their own right. But I think it is more helpful to think of understanding and meaning as relations between objects or subjects in the world and *ourselves*. The moment we can relate to them, they start to have meaning. And if we can define the relationship we have, or can even predict the behavior of the object, we understand it. For example, I

---

2 Also see "Medieval Best Practices"

understand how to drive a car; I can see how my actions relate to the behavior of the car while driving it. However, my understanding is more limited than the understanding of a mechanic, who can relate to putting the various components together.

The keyword in all this is "ourselves." Said another way, we need to be self-aware. Self-awareness means that we can be the objects of our own thoughts. We can reflect on our own being, characteristics, behaviors, thoughts and actions. We can step outside of ourselves and look at ourselves. This can be very shallow when we look in the mirror and decide we don't look that bad. Self-awareness can also go very deep, creating an understanding of who we truly are and what we believe in, and then we can consciously decide on how to behave. We have the will and power to stop intuitive reactions and behaviors and react the way we believe we should react, in a more appropriate manner. This is missing in this "can computers think" discussion so far.

So, can computers be self-aware? This has been an important theme in science fiction, at least. The *Terminator* movies describe the war between humanity and Skynet, a computer network so advanced that it became self-aware. The system engineers who designed Skynet realized the consequences and tried to shut it down. Skynet saw this as a threat to its own existence (realizing your own existence, and being able to grasp the concept of death are key concepts of self-awareness), and struck back – Judgment Day. Or consider *The Matrix* trilogy,[3] in which computers run the world and use comatose human bodies as batteries. It turns out that even Neo himself, escaping the dream world to live in the real world fighting the Matrix, is a product of the Matrix. The Matrix has the self-awareness to realize it needs an external stimulus to reinvent itself to

---

3 Arthur C. Clarke's "The City and the Stars" (1956) is a story that describes exactly the same dynamic as told in The Matrix. Alvin, a "unique" as it is called, is created to leave the city of Diaspar and explore.

become a better version of itself time and time again. In fact, every system that *realizes* it needs to renew itself in order to surive is self-aware.

In order to renew yourself, you need to be able to learn. And this is the argument that opponents always bring forward. A computer only does what it is told. The argument is easy to counter. IBM's Deep Blue played better chess than its programmers ever could. It learned so much about chess that it beat Garry Kasparov, the reigning world champion. IBM's Watson built so much knowledge that it beat the world champions on *Jeopardy!*. Fraud detection systems contain self-learning algorithms; in fact, self-learning is a complete branch in an IT discipline called data mining. Learning is the cognitive process of acquiring skill or knowledge, and very much the domain of computers.

Can computers rewrite their own programming? This would have to be part of computers renewing themselves. In fact, there is an established term for it: metamorphic code. It is a technique used in computer viruses in order to remain undetected. Most computer viruses are recognized by a certain footprint, a combination of code. By continuously changing it, computer viruses become harder to detect. Every generation the virus reproduces itself, it reproduces a slightly different, but still functioning version. In principle, this is not different from human evolution. You could call the self-evolution of computers, as witnessed through viruses, an early stage of evolution. It's far from the evolution the human race has experienced, but it is entirely conceivable computers will ultimately evolve to a similar or much more powerful organism than human beings. Given that the evolution takes place in the digital world, it is even likely this form of evolution goes infinitely faster than evolution in the real world.

In general, you can even argue computers can be self-aware in a much better way than human beings. Computers can make themselves the subject of their analysis completely dispassionately and objectively. They can run a self-diagnostic and report what they believe is malfunctioning in their system. Modern mathematics helps computers to judge the quality of their own program. Computers don't kid themselves like people do (when people are asked if they belong to the top 50% of students or drivers, invariably more than 50% rate themselves to be).

At the same time, dispassion is also the issue. How self-aware is the analysis then, if the analysis doesn't differentiate between itself and another computer in the outside world? It's not. Furthermore, can computers self-reflect on their self-reflection? Maybe, if they are programmed to do so, there can be a diagnostic of diagnostics. A meta diagnostic is not hard to imagine. But let's continue this. Could computers self-reflect on the self-reflection of their self-reflection?

Here we hit an interesting point. What does it mean to self-reflect on the self-reflection of your self-reflection? Most people would struggle with it, and that is exactly the point. This is why we human beings have invented the concept of the *soul*. The soul is the "metalevel of being" that we don't even grasp ourselves. So likewise, a computer doesn't have to fully understand itself to still be self-aware. After all, do we? Our brains are not capable of fully fathoming themselves. We can map what happens in our brain during all kinds of activities, but it doesn't mean we can truly understand it. By definition, we cannot step outside the paradigm in which we live. It is no use to theorize about what came before the Big Bang. The Big Bang created time, space and causality, and we need time, space and causality to think. Anything related to the absence of time, space and causality then is unthinkable. As such, a computer can't think outside of its own universe either.

I Think, Therefore I Am

In trying to think this through, perhaps we are approaching the matter from the wrong angle. As human beings, we feel superior to computers. We have created computers, so we are the computer's god. How could computers be better than we are? Every time we come to the conclusion, through reasoning, that conceptually computers are not very different from us –that they can think, and that they can be self-aware – we come up with a new reason why we are different. The killer argument is that computers do not create and invent things like we do. Computers haven't created any true art simply because they felt like it. Computers haven't displayed altruistic behavior. Computers don't make weird lateral thinking steps and invent Post-it Notes when confronted with glue that doesn't really stick, or invent penicillin by mistake.

And there we are… mistake. That is the keyword. We, human beings, are special because we are deeply flawed. We make mistakes, we don't always think rationally, our programming over many, many years of evolution is full of code that doesn't make any sense, and so forth. We are special because we are imperfect. In a paradoxical way, our superiority – today(!)– is in our imperfection. Because we don't know anything for sure, we have to keep trying to come up with better ways and better ideas. As long as we keep doubting ourselves (which only a self-aware person can), we improve and sustain our state of being.

For computers to pass the Turing test and become superior (at least from a human point of view), they need to take uncertainty into account. Computers have no issue with probabilistic reasoning, but should rely more on fuzzy interpretation.[4] To put it in provocative terms, they should become more imperfect. They should be able to doubt, be uncertain and reflect on their own thinking. From here it is only a small step to Descartes.

Rene Descartes (1596-1650), a French philosopher, tried to establish a fundamental set of principles of what is true.

---

4 Humans have a so-called mirror gene. If we see someone else cry, the center in our brain that controls crying is activated too. If someone else eats, we can become hungry too. In interpreting human behavior of others, we reach within ourselves. This is what computers don't have. Intelligence does not have to be human, but inhuman intelligence will have trouble interpreting human behavior.

He looked at phenomena and the world around him and asked if there were different explanations possible, a way of testing whether the existing explanations were correct. The safest way of asking these questions is to have no preconceptions at all, to doubt absolutely everything. The only way to establish truth is to reach a certain sound foundation or, in other words, an ontology from which the rest can be derived.

Descartes eventually reached the conclusion that everything can be doubted, except doubt itself. You cannot doubt your doubt because that would mean all would be certain, and that is what you are doubting. The thought of doubt itself proves that doubt cannot be doubted. And because you cannot separate a person from his thoughts, therefore, *cogito ergo sum*: I think (doubt), therefore I am.

If you doubt things, it means you are not sure. You are aware of your shortcomings to grasp the truth. And the only thing you can do to evolve your understanding is to doubt what you think you know. For computers to learn organically, break free of their programming and evolve, become creative, and be able to deal with unknown, unprogrammed situations,[5] computers need to become less perfect.

Turing would have loved the thought. Computers that can think, can doubt. So, computers that can truly think, at least in this definition, are to a certain extent unreliable. In fact, we can even take it a step further. To try to beat Deep Blue, Kasparov played a very intimidating game. Unfortunately, Deep Blue couldn't be intimidated, and it had no effect or at least not the effect it would have had on a human being. A really smart computer would have

_____
5 Although I don't really subscribe to this school of thinking, analytic philosophy comes to our aid again. There is an old story that tells how easy it was for the Europeans to conquer Native Americans. As the Native Americans did not have any concept for sailboats, and no words for it, they simply didn't register the sailboars at the horizon. It shows humans don't know how to deal with unprogrammed situations as much as we would like to believe we can.

been able to look beyond the chess board and interpret the behavior of the opponent. Interpretation is not an exact science. Sometimes interpretations are wrong. You could argue that only stupid computers win all the time. IBM's Deep Blue would have been *really* smart if it had been able to lose to Garry Kasparov, too.

Perhaps Google is actually a good example of the non-perfect computing paradigm. Google doesn't claim to have a single version of the truth, or to possess the ultimate knowledge and wisdom. On the contrary, *panta rhei*, as Heraclitus (535 – 475 BC) said, everything flows. Google's data basis is continuously changing, and googling for something twice might very well lead to two different results. Google also gives multiple answers, a non-exact response to usually pretty non-exact questions. Still, it's a pretty crude process. Some search engines use fuzzy logic and also search for information that is "round and about" what the user is asking for. If, for instance, you are looking for a second-hand Mercedes, preferably black, with not more than 50,000 miles on the odometer, the search engine may also return a dark blue Lexus with a mileage of 52,000.

Once we are the next generation down the road and the semantic Web becomes a reality, information retrieval and processing in general will become a bit more intelligent. On the semantic Web, computers will be able to understand the meaning of the information that flows around, based on ontological data structures. An ontology is a formal representation of knowledge as a set of concepts within a domain and the relationships between those concepts. If a human is formulating a search in an ambiguous way, search engines will be able to ask intelligent questions in order to provide a better result. Moreover, computers will be able to meaningfully process information without any human interaction or intervention.

Big Data and Big Process
Congratulations, dear reader, for coming this far in this essay. Mostly it has been intellectual play. And I didn't

even dive into singularity thinking, which predicts far-reaching coalescence between humans and machines. Is there any practical value to the whole discussion of whether computers can think? The answer might be more obvious than you would think.

We have confirmed that computers can think. A thought a computer may have is nothing else but everything it derives from processing data, such as a correlation, a segmentation, or any other type of step towards calculating a result. We have even confirmed that computers can be self-aware. Let's answer the following question: Can computers be individuals? Sure, they can be individualized, with all kinds of settings, but can computers have a mind of their own?

To get where I'd like to take this, we need to separate computer and content, which is impossible for human beings, but business as usual for computers operating in the cloud. For the purposes of determining if computers can be like individuals, we'll focus on large data sets.

The overload of information is growing, and it is potentially growing faster than computers and Internet infrastructure. *Big data* is one of the most significant trends in IT. If data sets become too big to be copied within reasonable time frames, you effectively cannot copy them anymore. They become unique. Data collections become *individuals* in the literal sense of the word: They exist just once. Two collections of data may be similar or related, like siblings, but can never be identical. Furthermore, their complexity in terms of volume, variety and velocity is so high it cannot be understood by normal human beings. With a little bit of imagination, you can argue that data sets become person-like.[6] They grow and mature over time. Data sets develop unique behaviors that they display when you interact with them. They could even develop dysfunctions and have disorders, being trained by the data and

---

6 I'd like to recognize Roland Rambau, a colleague of mine when I worked at Oracle, for coming up with this idea.

the analyses the systems perform.[7] The complexity makes it so that we simply have to trust the answers the systems give because the moment we try to audit the answers, the data has already changed. Effectively, like people, systems just offer a subjective point of view that is sometimes hard to verify.

In this scenario, information managers are further away from the "one version of the truth" they strive for than ever before. Perhaps information managers should leave their Era of Enlightenment behind. Perhaps the idea that there is a single truth, and all that needs to happen is to discover it and roll it out, is not realistic. Perhaps it is time for a new wave –the days of "postmodern information management."

Postmodernism, a term used in architecture, literature, and philosophy, has its roots in the late 19th century. Fronted by philosophers such as Martin Heidegger (1889–1976) and Michel Foucault (1926–1984), postmodernism has declared the "death of truth." Postmodernism is a reaction to the "modernist" and "enlightened" scientific approach to the world. According to postmodernists, reality is nothing more than a viewpoint, and every person has a different viewpoint. This means there are many realities. Reality is not objective, but subjective. And realities may very well conflict (something we notice in practical life every day as we sit in meetings discussing problems and solutions).

Although debated (which school of thought isn't?) and not the only trend in 20th century philosophy (analytic philosophers disagree fundamentally with postmodernists), I think it is safe to say that in the Western world, postmodernism is deeply entrenched in society. In a liberal and democratic world, we are all entitled to our opinions; and although some opinions are more equal than others, our individual voices are heard and have an influence in debates. (Except in information management.)

---

7 My career recommendation for the years to come is to become a "data therapist."

What would, for instance, postmodern "business intelligence" look like? If data sets are too complex for humans to fully understand where their responses come from, the answers they give can only be qualified as opinion. We can't verify the answer is correct. Their opinions, as unique individuals, may differ from the opinions of another data source. Managers need to think for themselves again and interpret the outcome of querying different sources, forming their particular picture of reality – not based on "the numbers that speak for themselves" or on fact-based analysis, but based on synthesizing multiple points of view to construct a story.

Just what would postmodern "business process management" look like? It would not be possible to define and document every single process that flows through our organization. After all, every instance of every process would be unique, the result of a specific interaction between you and a customer or any other stakeholder. What is needed is an understanding that different people have different requirements, and structure those in an ontological approach. In a postmodern world, we base our conversations on a meta-understanding. We understand that everyone has a different understanding.

Of course, as we do today, we can automate those interactions as well. Once we have semantic interoperability between data sets, processes, systems and computers in the form of master data management, metadata management, and communication standards based on XML (in human terms: "language"), systems can exchange viewpoints, negotiate, triangulate and form a common opinion. Most likely, given the multiple viewpoints, the outcome would be better than one provided by the traditional "single version of the truth" approach.

Thinking this through, could it be that postmodern information management and postmodern process management is here today? Could that be the reason why most "single version of the truth" approaches have failed so miserably over the last twenty (or more) years? Did reality already overtake the old IT philosophy? One thing is clear: Before we are able to embrace postmodernism in IT, we need to seriously re-architect our systems, tools, applications and methodologies.

Final Thought

In my mind, perhaps the ultimate test of whether computers can think is a variation on Turing's test. I pose the following question: Do computers have a sense of humor? This was the one thing Lt. Commander Data always struggled with in *Star Trek*. He had read everything about humor that was ever published, but still wasn't able to interpret the simplest joke.

Perhaps my computer has a sense of humor already in acting so weirdly today, but if that is the case, I simply don't get it.

Plato and the Art of IT Governance

"Until kings are philosophers and philosophers are kings, cities will never cease from ill."
- Plato

Why is IT governance such an important theme? Don't we have an organizational structure to govern business functions such as IT? Why are marketing governance or human resources governance much less of an issue? Don't we have a CIO whose job it is to govern IT? And don't we have an organizational structure with program managers, project managers on the development side, and administrators and support specialists on the maintenance side? Aren't there solid methodologies out there that help manage and govern work, such as Prince2 for designing, developing and implementing systems and ITIL for running and managing those systems? In fact, Cobit is a framework specifically developed for IT governance.

There are many definitions of IT governance (surprise, surprise), but I think the one that is most clear defines IT governance as "an integral part of corporate governance and addresses the definition and implementation of processes, structures and relational mechanisms in the organization that enable both business and IT people to execute their responsibilities in support of business/IT alignment and the creation of business value from IT enabled investments."

Although we have structures, jobs, processes and methodologies in place within the common practices of any organization, it doesn't seem to be enough, and IT governance continues to demand special attention. Why is this the case?

First, an obvious observation is that IT and business strategies enabled by IT have become so important for the survival and growth of the average organization that it warrants all the attention, as would any topic of that magnitude. Second, compared to other business functions such as finance, IT may still be less mature – just as governance of teenagers takes more time than governing adults. But there is another reason in an area where IT may even have a leading position: Perhaps more than in any other business function, IT operates in a stakeholder network.

As with any other support organization, IT has all the other business departments as stakeholders. IT also often has the lead in external stakeholder management. There are many parties with which IT needs to work, such as in outsourcing, consulting partners, value chain integration and so forth. The moment other business functions, such as finance, start outsourcing their operations (e.g., to a shared service center) governance becomes a special concern too.

Similar to the way feudal societies, centrally led by the elite, had trouble with democratic structures, organizations – managed through the hierarchy – have trouble managing stakeholder networks. An organization is not a group of agents with a common goal, but a unique collaboration between stakeholders to serve the goals of all. At least, that is one possible business philosophy. Let's see what the old philosophers have to say about IT governance. We turn to Plato.

Plato (427 BC - 347 BC) was a Greek philosopher, mathematician and the founder of the Academy in Athens, Greece. The Academy was the first university in the Western world. Plato's name is often combined with those of Socrates, Plato's master, and Aristotle, one of Plato's students, and they are seen as the most important contributors to the foundations of Western philosophy. In his book *The Republic*, Plato proves to be no fan of democracy. He felt democracy would lead to anarchy, and anarchy would lead to tyranny. Democracy in those days wasn't defined as it is today. Democracy was characterized as a system in which all qualifying citizens could gather in the Assembly and vote on issues. Today we call that a direct democracy. Perhaps Switzerland and the state of California, with their system of referenda, come closest to a direct democracy. Plato felt that the wisdom of crowds would lead to average and short-term decisions, and that democracy would not offer a strong future-focused vision. Plato described how democratic self-government wouldn't work, comparing governing a state to being the captain of a ship:

"Imagine then a ship or a fleet in which there is a captain who is taller and stronger than any of the crew, but who is a little deaf and has a similar infirmity in sight, and whose knowledge of navigation is not much better. The sailors are quarreling with one another about the steering – everyone is of the opinion that he has a right to steer, though he has never learned the art of navigation ..."

Plato felt that average citizens should not be allowed to run the state because they would not have the knowledge of economics, warfare, ethics and legal issues. Maybe this is one of the reasons why most modern societies are indirect democracies, where we vote for professional politicians who are supposed to have that knowledge and experience. If they turn out to be the wrong leaders, they get voted out. We agree with Plato's premise in business as well, but in a different way. Businesses leaders are not appointed by popular vote; in fact, it often takes a long career before someone moves into the C-level suite. In fact, Plato describes that career.

According to Plato, every child, male or female, should have the same education. This basic education should consist of gymnastics to train the body and music to feed the soul. After this basic education, children should be acquainted with mathematics, dialectics, and endurance. Endurance would consist of training on how to withstand temptation and pain, for example. When the students reach age twenty, there would be a first selection of those who would pass to the next round. The ones that pass continue their education for another ten years, followed by another selection. The next round of training, an additional five years, would be in philosophy. If you do the math, after those five years the remaining people are 35 years old, which is good but still not old and wise enough. For the remaining people, there is another 15 years in which they would be trained to lead in practical life. Today we would call that job rotation. Then, those who survive this last fifteen years would be appointed to senior leadership functions at the age of 50. This is not very different from the career path of professionals moving up the business hierarchy. It ensures that the vast majority of people who are not able to govern a business do not progress through all levels of training.

Plato also comments on the various tasks of the state. The basis is to supply food and other necessities to sustain its population. The state should also provide a defensive mechanism against enemies. Lastly, the state should govern, particularly through objective reasoning. It is amazing how this matches the typical IT stack. The IT organization supplies business applications and IT infrastructure to run the necessary processes. Then there is an IT operations layer, in which systems management, backups, security and other protective measures are taken, and then there is an analytic layer in the form of business intelligence systems.

Plato assigns different castes or classes for each task. There is the working class, consisting of skilled people of all trades. They represent the majority of society. However, soldiers need to protect the working class and all other members of society. And then there is the ruling class, who are rational, intelligent, self-controlled and well suited to make decisions for the community. Plato compares those three classes with part of the soul. The working class represents "appetite," the soldiers are the "spirit" and the governing class forms the "reason" of the soul.[1]

---

1 Plato briefly singles out traders as a group of people in society, and he is not very positive about them. For Plato, trade represented almost the lowest of activities. Software and hardware vendors might recognize that sentiment when negotiating deals with IT procurement professionals.

Again, it is possible to draw the parallel to the typical IT organization. The working class are the developers and specialists who bring in knowledge about different fields of IT. The administrators are the soldiers, as they protect the integrity of the data and the systems. Unfortunately, in business life, administrators have a slightly less heroic profile. But, in fact, this class is greatly expanding, following the IT trend of outsourcing activities. Outsourcing companies need to be managed as well, and complete outsourcing governance departments are established. The ruling class consists of the CIO, the IT managers and the analysts, who determine what the specialists and administrators should do next.

Plato had some other, more peculiar, views on the ideal state as well. Plato believed in a rather communistic and sectarian way that the soldiers should not have possessions, and that women and children were to be raised in common. Soldiers of the state should live together too, receiving no pay, just food. Families, children, slaves and possessions were for the working class. Soldiers should not have much to lose, or viewed from a different angle, should not have anything other than warfare to worry about.

Somehow I think most of us are pretty happy this vision has never become a reality, but there is a striking parallel with IT governance when discussing where the IT budget resides.

It is clear Plato would have frowned on the IT department managing its own budget. The best reason for IT to own its own budget is the belief that the people who have the most in-depth knowledge about IT, namely the IT department itself, are the best guarantee that the best decisions on how to spend the budget are taken. However, the moment IT owns the budget, IT itself, particularly when it acts as a service to the business, has a vested interest and starts to protect the budget for the sake of the budget.

So what is the alternative? Should the specific lines of business – the IT "customers"– own the budget in a decentralized manner? After all, the lines of business are the subject of IT expenditures. Aligning customer requirements with the willingness to spend makes sure nothing unnecessary is being built, and that projects will get the proper attention. Projects will also be tightly managed by the business. Then again, Plato would be quick to point out, if the lines of business own the IT budget, short-termism is the result, full of tactical solutions and lacking an overall infrastructure. An architecturally sound landscape with economies of scale and a high level of reusability would be unlikely.

That means there is only one option left: having the budget managed by senior management, but there are some drawbacks there as well. There are many other priorities, and the current generation of CEOs is not as IT-literate as they should be. Furthermore, IT decision making on this level would invite many political games, instead of what Plato envisioned: putting knowledge and reason in command.

Still, Plato would prefer having senior management decide, but based on solid IT knowledge and background. This should be fixed first. In The Republic, Plato wrote the following famous line:

"Until kings are philosophers and philosophers are kings, cities will never cease from ill."

Plato, the philosopher, feels that philosophers should be king, or – as we discussed already – the ruling class should have a solid background in philosophy.

Boy, would the enterprise architects love that. They would best qualify to be the CIOs of the future. In Plato's definition, philosophers are those who are capable of comprehending ideas, and are especially interested in the idea of good.[2] The enterprise architects come closest to a

---

2 "The idea of good" is something entirely different than "a good idea." The two should not be confused.

philosophical view on the business. They have developed how the business structures should look, which controls are needed and how the supporting IT should be architected. I bet that deep down many enterprise architects have felt they were the only ones who truly understood how the business is running, or at least have felt frustration when witnessing the decision makers in action, doing "silly things."[3]

Plato is on their side. Plato particularly recommends studying abstract mathematics as a preparation for the abstract conception of good. Any enterprise architect would agree.

But there is more to IT leadership than understanding what is good and understanding the full business consequences of architectural choices. Sometimes being a CIO is a dirty job indeed.

The Machiavellian CIO

Like many philosophers, Plato focuses on the ideal situation, describing his utopia. The aim is to discover truth, describe beauty and reach a perfect situation. But let's look at the definition of IT governance again, at least the last part: "... to enable both business and IT people to execute their responsibilities in support of business/IT alignment and the creation of business value from IT enabled investments."

This is not only about truth and beauty, but about reality – about being responsible for certain results and getting things done. This requires pragmatism and insight into how things work in practice. The type of philosophy that describes the perfect world doesn't suffice; a different type of philosophy is needed as well. Here we encounter the unavoidable Machiavelli and Sun Tzu.

---

3 In case you are an enterprise architect, and you catch yourself with the thought you are the only one who really gets it, ask yourself when was last time you negotiated a multiyear contract with a customer or supplier, taking customer requirements, your own profitability and revenue recognition regulations into account. Quickest way to wake up.

Niccolò di Bernardo de Machiavelli (1469–1527) was a diplomat and administrator in Florence during the Renaissance. He didn't have an easy life. Italian city-states were at constant war with each other, in varying coalitions, and with many shifts in power. Machiavelli fell from grace at one point as well, was tortured and lived in exile. It was during this period that he did most of his writing. Machiavelli's most famous book is called *The Prince*, and it deals with the difficulties of new princes gaining and sustaining power, including best practices in strategy, leadership, and how to use force and deceit. In short, it is good advice for every new executive in the corner-office, if not in applying Machiavelli's work, then at least in recognizing others doing it.

Despite the era it is written in, it is a surprisingly easy and sometimes amusing read. In fact, more recently, some have commented The Prince should be read as a work of irony, with Machiavelli meaning the opposite. Meant seriously or not, "being Machiavellian" today has a strong negative connotation. It stands for about every unfair way to reach your goals. If you set this current interpretation aside, what remains after reading The Prince and Machiavelli's other works, is a remarkable practical philosophy. Machiavelli doesn't describe how politics *should* work, he describes how they *do* work.

For instance, Machiavelli describes how to control occupied territory:

"In maintaining armed men there in place of colonies one spends much more, having to consume on the garrison all the income of the state, so that the acquisition turns into a loss, and many more are exasperated, because the whole state is injured; through the shifting of the garrison up and down."

This is directly applicable advice for CIOs. Even today, IT is sometimes housed at a separate location, leading to garrisons moving up and down. Collecting systems requirements from a distance, Machiavelli says, is much less productive and much more expensive. Instead, IT should be extremely close to the business and blend in IT should send its own citizens and let them live within the colony called business, creating harmony. If business and IT are one, business/IT alignment simply stops being an issue. Machiavelli continues:

"There never was a new prince who has disarmed his subjects; rather when he has found them disarmed he has always armed them, because, by arming them, those arms become yours, those men who were distrusted become faithful, and those who were faithful are kept so, and your subjects become your adherents."

In other words, keep your users happy. Empower them with the infrastructure to do things themselves; don't prescribe all solutions. Of course, there are areas of standardization (e.g., everything in finance), but in general the users should be empowered. How many new CIOs started doing that, instead of coming in and making a mark by strong standardization? Machiavelli describes the latter approach as follows:

"When you disarm them, you at once offend them by showing that you distrust them, either for cowardice or for want of loyalty, and either of these opinions breeds hatred against you."

In short, dear CIO, this is what happens if you go for a large centralized system as the first thing in your new job ;-).

The most important task of the CIO is to defend the IT territory:

"A prince who does not understand the art of war, over and above the other misfortunes already mentioned, cannot be respected by his soldiers, not can he rely on them. He ought never, therefore, to have out of his thoughts the subject of war, and in peace he should addict himself more to its exercise than in war; this he can do in two ways, the one by action, the other by study [...] A prince ought to have no other aim or thought, nor select anything

else for his study, than war and its rules and discipline; for this is
the sole art that belongs to him who rules, and it is of such force
that it not only upholds those who are born princes, but it often
enables men to rise from a private station to that rank. And, on
the contrary, it is seen that when princes have thought more of
ease than of arms they have lost their status. And the first cause
of your losing it is to neglect this art; and what enables you to
acquire a state is to be master of the art."

So much for philosophers being kings, and kings being philosophers!
Machiavelli is not the only one describing the grim reality of power and politics. Sun Tzu, an ancient Chinese military general and author of The Art of War has as well. Sun Tzu and Machiavelli make many of the same points. It is peculiar though that Machiavelli now has a bad reputation, while quoting Sun Tzu is considered to be a sign of strength and wisdom: "Business is war!"

Historians question if Sun Tzu was indeed an authentic historical figure, and when exactly he lived, either in the period of 544-496 BC, or somewhere between 476-221 BC. A well-known story describes the world in which Sun Tzu lived. The King of Wu wanted to test Sun Tzu's leadership skills, and asked him to train a group of 180 harem ladies to become soldiers. Sun Tzu started by appointing the two concubines most favored by the king as his officers, and gave them the "face, right" command. They giggled. He then repeated the order, as the general – in this case, Sun Tzu himself – is responsible for making sure orders are well understood. The concubines giggled again, and Sun Tzu had them executed. The king protested, but Sun Tzu explained that his officers have to obey, and that the task of the general is to carry out his mission, regardless of any complaint. Sun Tzu then appointed two new officers. His two officers and the other concubines performed perfectly. Governance!

Although Machiavelli and Sun Tzu have much in common, they each wrote in a different style. Machiavelli uses many historical examples and elaborate prose. The work of Sun Tzu is structured more like a list of instructions or short descriptions; what today we would call *best practices*.

Sun Tzu has many quotes that tell us a bit about governance. Management of many is the same as management of few; it is a matter of organization, he wrote. His definition of governance is much shorter than the one I have been using in this essay so far:

"Know your enemy and know yourself and you can fight a hundred battles without disaster."

In the case of IT, to be successful you need to be close to the business:

"It is said that if you know your enemies and know yourself, you will not be imperiled in a hundred battles; if you do not know your enemies but do know yourself, you will win one and lose one; if you do not know your enemies nor yourself, you will be imperiled in every single battle."

Sun Tzu also tells us to be analytical. His insight here is surprisingly fresh. The military method starts with measurement, and one should concentrate on measuring tangible and concrete things like distance, temperature and other factors affecting battle conditions. After measurement comes estimation of quantity, and Sun Tzu means the interpretation of the data to create meaningful information. Calculation comes third, which translates into creating an overview of your options to respond. Then comes the balancing of chances, which is an evaluation of what the best course of action is, based on the list of options available and the risks associated with them. Victory comes last. If I had attributed this list of five steps to Kaplan and Norton, who invented the balanced scorecard, you would have believed it too.

Sun Tzu also tells us to be dispassionate about control as part of governance, not be sidetracked by vested interests of others, and keep your eye on the goal. Hence,

"What is essential in war is victory, not prolonged operations."

IT believers will also recognize the idea of having a competitive edge through IT by adopting the principle of first mover advantage. In the case of Sun Tzu, though, it needs to be taken very literally:

"Whoever is first in the field and awaits the coming of the enemy, will be fresh for the fight; whoever is second in the field and has to hasten to battle will arrive exhausted. Appear at points which the enemy must hasten to defend; march swiftly to places where you are not expected. An army may march great distances without distress, if it marches through country where the enemy is not."

An angle to IT governance I haven't touched on so far is architecture. In hindsight it seems better to credit Sun Tzu for describing the principles of a service-oriented architecture first:

"There are not more than five musical notes, yet the combinations of these five give rise to more melodies than can ever be heard. There are not more than five primary colors (blue, yellow, red, white, and black), yet in combination they produce more hues than can ever been seen. There are not more than five cardinal tastes (sour, acrid, salt, sweet, bitter), yet combinations of them yield more flavors than can ever be tasted."

But we shouldn't forget being successful is still a dirty job. I am not sure if we can call Sun Tzu Machiavellian in nature, as Machiavelli wasn't born yet, but let there be no mistake:

"All warfare is based on deception. Hence, when we are able to attack, we must seem unable; when using our forces, we must appear inactive; when we are near, we must make the enemy believe we are far away; when far away, we must make him believe

we are near. Hold out baits to entice the enemy. Feign disorder,
and crush him."

Leadership lessons

So far we've had some fun with Plato, Machiavelli and Sun Tzu, making some serious – and some less serious – points. When going through Plato's ideas on governance, I felt something was missing. Plato may have a point that it is better for a soldier not to have a family, but it is a very rational, technocratic view. Plato is lacking the human view. Machiavelli and Sun Tzu spend a surprisingly large part of their time discussing the human side: the characteristics of a prince or a general, and on building relationships. This is as equally important as having the right strategy, the right organization and the right mechanisms. For instance, Machiavelli elaborates on how to avoid being despised and hated as a prince, in order to survive. And Sun Tzu writes:

"Regard your soldiers as your children, and they will follow you into the deepest valleys; look upon them as your own beloved sons, and they will stand by you even unto death."

These are leadership lessons! They are about behavior. They provide a much deeper insight into governing your environment. In the Western world, the philosophy that has had the most impact on leadership behavior is stoicism. Developed by Zeno of Citium (c. 334-262 B.C.), the history books say that stoicism had its influence until deep into the days of the Roman Empire, especially the years of Marcus Aurelius (121-180 B.C.).[4] I would argue that stoicism is still the dominant philosophy in management and leadership today. In fact, the description of stoicism reads like a definition of Jim Collins' "Level 5 Leadership." The fundamental principle of stoicism is that in order to find true happiness,

---

4 You may remember Marcus Aurelius leading the troops on campaign in Germany in the first act of the movie Gladiator

we should be free of all emotions and passions. Pain only becomes painful, if we consider pain a negative emotion. According to the stoics, everything in the world is predestined, and our freedom and autonomy consists of how we react to it. The measure of a person is not in what he says, but in how he behaves. A true stoic is serene and elevated above everything that happens in the world – unshaken.

The first true stoic that comes to mind is Mr. Spock, from Star Trek. He is unshakable, courageous, disciplined, and highly ethical. Isn't this how most C-level executives like to portray themselves as well? No matter how big the crisis, they act calm, cool and collected. In meetings, they keep their cards close to their chests, and don't show any signs of emotion. It's all business. We also appreciate stoic characters in public office. In fact, Barack Obama qualifies as a good one. Stoicism is not about suppressing emotion, though (that by itself would be failing the test); it is about truly understanding what is within our circle of influence and control, focusing on that, and not getting worked up about anything outside that circle. It should be said that stoicism differs greatly from cynicism (in establishing stoic philosophy, Zeno actually reacts on the philosophy of the cynics). Cynics believe in egoism, and they put their own interests in the center. Stoics, on the contrary, deeply value friendship, believe in justice and are philanthropic in nature. Even barbarians and slaves are accepted as equals. (Now that is something corporate executives should realize when mirroring themselves to the stoics!) It is also good for top managers to know that stoics are indifferent to possession and honor.

With the exception of Machiavelli and perhaps a few other schools of thought, the human perspective is generally lacking in Western philosophy, which is all logic and reason. Western philosophy predominantly focuses on the "what" and "why" of things, taking an analytic and rational approach. It looks at the world in terms of structures and searches for the ultimate truth.

In Eastern philosophy, there is more room for the "how"

question, i.e., how to make the most out of reality in a very practical sense, such as looking at the world in terms of relationships and allowing ambiguity. It is less analytical (trying to categorize everything), and more synthetic (connecting things). In fact, ancient Chinese philosophy still has a huge impact on Eastern society today, especially Confucianism and Taoism. Confucius (551-479 B.C.) is more for the common people, explaining how to live a humble and practical life, and honoring traditions. Lao Tse (6th century B.C), the assumed father of Taoism, focuses more on the elite, stating that leading an honorable life is not for everyone. Taoism says that the right way is leading by example. Without too many words, laws, regulations and commandments, a ruler needs to govern by showing his own quiet and virtuous life. The more rules there are, the poorer the people will be, as rules kill entrepreneurial spirit. As with stoicism, you should come to conclusions based on reason.[5] This is the only virtue on the path to success. Being unreasonable is the only sin.

Now that's powerful advice when thinking about governance – reason as the center of success, not mechanisms, processes and structures. In the end, we all know this. In my consulting career I learned that reorganization is the last resort in change management. First, work on the behaviors of people, then change their activities. Only if that doesn't work, look into processes and organization. But we keep falling in the trap of reorganizing for better governance, because it is the rational and objective thing to do, as well as the easiest. But is it the best way of organizing governance? No, not really.

To Govern or to be Governed, That is the Question

I wouldn't be surprised if research showed that most governance problems are not caused by a lack of process, structures and mechanisms of governance, but for other reasons. For instance, a lack of alignment between gov-

---

5 Being reasonable doesn't necessarily equal being rational.

ernance principles and the real world (too much Plato, not enough Machiavelli), or equally likely, because of political games, dysfunctional behaviors and people putting their own goals before the organizational goals.

Let's make a comparison between an organization and a society. Philosophers such as Thomas Hobbes (1588-1679) and John Locke (1632-1704) have argued that creating a state is not a top-down exercise, in those times described as a given by God. A society is the result of a social contract between citizens, who prefer handing over some natural rights to a government rather than a state of nature in which everyone has to fight for their own survival. As Hobbes stated, life without a social contract would be "nasty, brutal and short."

Employment is very much the same way. Although business futurists for years now have advocated for everyone in the brave new world to be self-employed, going from one project to the next, most employees prefer a safe employment over the anarchy of the open market and a nasty, brutal and short career trying to make some money here and there. Entrepreneurship simply isn't for everyone. Classical organizational theory even defines a salary in the same terms as a social contract. For the benefit of receiving a salary, employees give up the pursuit of their own goals, at least for the number of working hours per day, and they have a boss to tell them what to do.

But obviously, it doesn't work that way anymore. We can all attest to that. There must be another angle that we haven't discussed yet. So far we have discussed how to govern and often that is all that is discussed in corporate life. But Confucius brings up a good point. What about the opposite; what about how to be governed? The numerous employees working across the organization play a role too.

Locke and Hobbes already defined the social contract as a bottom-up principle, instead of society being imposed top-down. But it wasn't until the twentieth century, around the 1980s, when the idea of looking at society from a public-debate-in-small-communities point of view emerged. Or should I say re-emerge, as this is how Plato described a direct democracy in the Greek city-states. Politics is too important to leave to the politicians, the communitarians would say. Communitarianism emphasizes the need to balance individual rights and interests with that of the community as a whole, and argues that individual people (or citizens) are shaped by the cultures and values of their communities. Two prominent communitarians are Michael Sandel (1953), philosophy professor at Harvard, and Amitai Etzioni (1929), director of the Institute for Communitarian Policy Studies at George Washington University.

Communitarianism is an interesting angle to explore to get new insights into governance for two reasons. First, unbridled capitalism, the view that business is amoral, and the lack of a sense of community have been causing severe societal and business disruption in recent years. So any examination could be helpful in improving business governance. Second, communitarian thinking very much aligns with the 2.0 trend in business and technology.

Sandel sees a more important role for solidarity, social responsibility and a general sense of community. Translated to business, this would lead to a different view on governance. The following principles read like an "Anything 2.0" manual:

- Communitarians don't believe in top-down rules, but rely on the assumed wisdom and experience of a community that has a strong and distinct culture.
- Citizens should not only know their rights, but particularly their responsibilities. Citizens should involve themselves in society because they feel a sense of ownership and care for the society in which they belong.
- Communitarianism leans heavily on mutual communication within the community. Within the tight structure of the family, the church or other social structures it is easier to keep people on the straight path.
- Sometimes privacy and other personal goals are sub-

jected to other, higher purposes, serving the whole community.

Is this back to the old days? The moral society of the 1950s? On the contrary; it is pure 2.0 thinking. The current generation that has entered the workforce, called Generation Y (people born after 1980), are collaborative in nature, expect decision-making to be a group process and seek advice from their peers more than from their superiors. Today already the impact of the use of social networks within business can hardly be overestimated.

So what does this all mean for IT governance within business? Let's recall part of the definition of IT governance: "... addresses the definition and implementation of processes, structures and relational mechanisms in the organization..." From a communitarian point of view, these processes, structures and mechanisms shouldn't come from management and shouldn't be imposed on all employees. Instead, good governance would be facilitating a company-wide ongoing discussion on what is right and wrong. Good governance would be governance on the metalevel: creating a process that creates the process. The definition of governance would come out of the group, but also the enforcement of it. The role of management is to facilitate the process and make sure the right people are involved.

But be careful what you wish for, because it might come true. It does sound like a dream come true for employees, as their voices are finally heard and they become an integral part of the organization's strategic process. But with great freedom comes great responsibility. Employees also become accountable, and through 2.0 technology the community discussion is transparent. Brilliant ideas are visible to everyone, as well as less brilliant ideas. And not participating in the process is also very visible. In fact, everything you do and don't do becomes uncomfortably visible. With hierarchic boundaries removed, every voice competes with all others. It becomes a step back to the state of nature – survival of the fittest.

It would also be foolish to assume that an enterprise 2.0

would no longer need management and would become self-organizing. In fact, I would argue that in the 2.0 world, management and leadership skills become even more important. It requires wisdom and a lot of experience to moderate communication and decision-making processes in such a way that everyone has been able to contribute, that there is buy-in from everyone, that the topic of discussion is aligned with other topics, that all external aspects such as regulations are considered as well, and that the result is both in time and practical. In fact, in Plato's terms, it would take a philosopher king to manage such a process.

The communitarian view raises the stakes for management in other ways too. I am not even addressing the fear of letting go, and hoping the discussion goes in the right direction. Moderating discussion is a management task anyway, whether it is in the 2.0 world or not. No, I am addressing a much more fundamental issue: the true nature of governance.

Governance in practice today is often not much more than "organizing compliance." Making sure the company obeys all Sarbanes-Oxley regulations, industry-specific rule, and other legal requirements. Fundamentally, as hard as it is, it is a tick-in-the-box-exercise. Compliance is like being a child: cleaning up your room because you have to.

I believe the definition of governance we've been using is missing the point. Governance is like being a grown-up: running a decent household because you want to, and because it serves the purposes of everyone in the family. Governance communitarian style is about what is right and what is wrong, according to the values and culture of the organization. It's about the strategic principles and how they affect the entire organization. It is governance as we would define it in our personal lives, e.g., governing ourselves as human beings, composing ourselves, controlling ourselves in difficult situations, questioning and analyzing our own behavior. We behave ourselves because we want to, not because we should. A challenging perspective indeed.

Technology: Can't Live with It, Can't Live without It

"Customer service has never been as bad as since the advent of CRM systems."

Recently I bought a train ticket at a machine, using my credit card. The procedure was aborted by the machine: "Unusable Card," it said. Unusable? I had just bought a sandwich with it, and it was quite usable yesterday too, thank you very much. The machine should have said, "I am terribly sorry for failing in the single task I am actually supposed to do, but I can't seem to read your card."

Ironically, when I was sharing my frustration about the machine with someone on the phone, we got disconnected. A metallic voice told me, "Your call has been completed." Excuse me? My call wasn't completed at all. It was terminated. That is what the voice should have said.

Examples are all around us. In business, it seems like customer service has never been as bad as since the advent of CRM (customer relationship management) systems. The moment your case is not covered by the scripts and business rules locked into the system, customer self-service systems built for "straight-through processing" can't help you anymore. Good luck. Try to find a phone number on the website somewhere. Even if you are lucky enough to speak with a real person on the phone, chances are that call center agent won't be able to help you either, restricted by the same business rules and systems.

Both examples are typical results of *engineering thinking*, reasoning from within the system. Everything outside of the rules of the system is seen as an anomaly, a.k.a. the real world. Much attention is being paid to user interfaces and interaction, but if the designers live within the confines of their own systems instead of in the world of the users, they will create silly responses that annoy users. Are we in control of the technology we use, or are we already under control?

Engineering Thinking and Ambient Computing

I think we are getting used to it. We think in terms of how to work the system and how to beat the system. Users are reduced to operators of the system. Using our smart-phones to organize our lives by organizing the systems that support us has become a second nature, our new reality. Even worse, the systems around us organize us. Advanced analytics decide which advertisements we see, try to predict which movies and what music we like, and which discount coupons we get in the supermarket to entice us to try a new type of salad dressing. Additionally, it is a self-reinforcing loop. Smart systems determining customer segmentations present people with choices within a particular segment. Because there is so much choice, chances are we rely on the choices presented, confirming the segmented picture the system has of us and strengthening our – in essence already predetermined – profile.

These types of advanced analytics represent the opposite of engineering thinking, in which we need to understand how a system works. The goal of *ambient computing* is that you never even see the system. It just functions in the background. Although IT is still dominated by engineering thinking, ambient computing is the "new way to go." On the infrastructure level, cloud computing is a good example. We really don't have to care anymore where data and applications reside. We just use them on a device of choice.

Cloud computing is perhaps the easiest part of the equation because it is "only" infrastructure. We don't really have to see it because it has no user interface. Computers still have significant issues interpreting our behavior and trying to adapt to it. Most users of the latest version of Microsoft Office become accustomed to the ribbons, where you only see the buttons associated with the type of work you do. That seems to work pretty well, but have you ever tried to make an Apple device do what you want it to do, slightly outside the normal routine? Impossible. User friendliness goes hand in hand with loss of control. Most advanced photocopiers have the same issue. These copiers recognize paper size automatically, so copying the upper half of a letter-sized paper sideways is simply not possible anymore. Or think of the autocorrect software in your smartphone that suggests words as shortcuts and the embarrassing results this can lead to.[1] As much as engineering thinking, ambient computing leads to frustration in working with systems and computers.

So I ask, forgive me the gloomy thoughts, are we in control of our technology, or are we already under control of technology? Is technology liberating us from chores we don't like to do, or has IT become the ultimate prison?

Technology and Real Life Have Blended

In any case, we have come to depend on technology in most aspects of our life. In fact, we feel uncomfortable without. How many telephone numbers do you still know without checking your phone? How many times do you use a navigation system, even if you are relatively confident you know how to get to your destination? Have you had a slight panic attack because you forgot your phone or your computer power cable on a small trip? And I keep wondering what would happen worldwide if Facebook would be down for a week…

The real world and the virtual world are interconnected to such an extent that sometimes it is difficult to distinguish where one begins and the other ends. Indeed, friendships would be different without Facebook. People find new meaningful relationships using dating sites. Young adults applying for jobs rightfully claim leadership skills based on their experience with World of Warcraft. Second Life became so big for a time that it had its own economy, and tax services were considering how to deal with that.

This is only the beginning. We already can imagine the next wave of medical technology evolution. Medical technology is currently in the engineering phase with external, visible technology such as hearing aids and internal, but self-sufficient technology such as pacemakers. What happens if medical technology goes ambient and becomes biotechnology? Imagine how technology will affect us if it

---

1 www.damnyouautocorrect.com is full of embarrassing examples

starts to communicate with our brains.

Rene Descartes (1596-1650) said that science should be a benefit to all and should serve progress. It should take care of menial tasks, making labor easier, and it should be useful in social life too. Substitute science with technology, and you have a very modern definition of what technology should do. Technology is meant to amplify human abilities,[2] such as sight, strength, speed and so forth. Examples of this amplification through technology include the Internet (sight), drilling machines (strength) and cars (speed).

The more we use technology, the more we depend on it. This comes with some good cause for concern as well. For instance, what about our safety if something goes wrong? You could almost formulate a law here, the *law of the constant impact*. It would go something like this: The more we rely on technology, and the more reliable technology becomes (which means the chance of technology breaking down decreases), the higher the impact should it break down. Probability times impact is a constant. As private persons, businesses and society as a whole, we rely on Internet connectivity and trust it will work when we need it. We simply cannot work in those (rare) cases it is not available. Many of us rely so heavily on our navigation systems that we don't feel comfortable going somewhere without. Many countries relied on nuclear energy technology until the nuclear disaster in Japan in 2011, but are now questioning their continued reliance on this type of energy.

Another concern is environmental. It is wonderful we have so much technology at our disposal, but what do we do with the millions and millions of old phones and the billions of old sensors we'll see appearing in the years to come? How will the environment be affected by the CO_2 emissions from producing all the needed technology?

What about privacy? We care so much for our Facebook accounts that we allow Facebook to store and use everything it knows about us. We appreciate the ease of use of our navi-

2 Also see "Technology, What Have You Done for Me Lately?"

gation systems, even though the providers can sell aggregated data from these systems to the police to plan speed traps.

To Use or Not to Use – That is the question

While technology is a benefit for all and does serve progress, there are serious concerns related to technology and its use. The consequentialist will take this relatively light-heartedly. The question of whether the benefits outweigh the concerns lies not in the technology itself, but in its use. Technology itself is amoral of nature. Universalists would be more interested to explore benefits and concerns prior to using a certain technology. They would feel the need to take a stance on what's right and what's wrong up front.

There's something to be said for both views; it is easy to see both have a point. But both points of view have their challenges too. Take, for instance, the development of nuclear or biological weapons. It would be too easy for the consequentialists to say that whether having weapons like this is good or bad depends on what you do with them. The best thing you can say about weapons of mass destruction is that they would scare off any potential enemy, but is that sufficient justification? Furthermore, you can't really undo knowledge. Once it is there, it is there and you're going to have to live with it. All in all, not the strongest of value propositions.

Universalists would point out that these weapons are designed and produced with a true possibility of actually use. And if one would use them, this would trigger someone else to use them as well, triggering others to use them too. This would likely lead to end of humanity. This cannot be good; therefore, we should not have weapons of mass destruction.[3] But can we stop technological progress? Should we stop technological and scientific re-

---

3 This reasoning is an example of Kant's "categorizal imperative." This is a rational examination of the intentions behind actions. If you believe that everyone should do what you do, then an action can be called good. If you believe not everyone should do the same, think about your intended action again.

search at some point because, for instance, biological warfare and stem cell research are deemed unethical? Is there knowledge we simply shouldn't have? A good question to ask at face value, but I find the question a bit too simplistic. Technology innovation is seldom a linear path. Many elements of nuclear technology and biotechnology were invented without the idea of warfare in mind. So what's there to decide up front?

Dilemmas like this may look larger than life, but we can see them on a smaller scale as well. Take, for instance, Apple's decision to lock iPhones to work only with certain telecom service providers and to not allow Flash technology on the iPad. Or consider Microsoft integrating Internet Explorer so deeply into Windows that other browsers could not work effectively and efficiently on a Windows-based computer. If you consider business and the market to be amoral, there is nothing against decisions like this. It allows Apple to keep full control over both the business model and the technology in use, and present a consistent image to the market. Consequentialists will point out that the decision as such is not an issue unless Apple made those decisions with the express purpose to harm a competitor, without having the best interest of the customer in mind. Universalists may rightfully point out that this harmful effect is built into the design decision itself, leading to unethical consequences per definition.

Sometimes regulators and governments solve the issue. Microsoft was forced to allow users to choose a browser, and iPhone "jailbreaks" to unlock the phone are not illegal. Sometimes the market takes care of it. One of the competitive differentiators of Android-based tablets is that they support the Flash-world.

Slowly and surely, we've reached a few interesting conclusions. The first conclusion is that weighing the benefits and the risks of humanity's dependence on technology is essentially an *ethical debate*. In other words, making sure that technology benefits all and serves progress is a guide for "doing the right thing."

The second conclusion is that both the consequential-ist and the universalist approach lead to important dilemmas. Dilemmas often come up as a result of constraints. It is difficult to offer the highest quality and also be the cheapest in the market. It is hard to offer an open technology platform while keeping full control over the user experience. It is hard to find a medical cure that doesn't have any side effects. These are constraints that force us to make choices, when we would prefer to have both, at the same time.

Harnessing Innovation Through More Knowledge

However, this is where technology innovation comes to the rescue. Innovation can be defined as the art of lifting constraints. The Sony walkman lifted a constraint called "size." It made it possible to pick up a tape recorder and make it portable. MP3 players, a few steps later in the same line of innovation, eliminated the capacity constraints so you don't have to choose what music to bring. MP3 players also eliminated a stability constraint, allowing people to run while listening to music in high quality. In business, service-oriented architectures and model-driven applications eliminate the need to choose between standard functionality, while servicing your unique requirements. Internet technology dramatically reduced transaction costs, which allows organizations to outsource activities, improving both quality and price. No choice between the two is needed anymore.

These constraints are all material, physical constraints. It is only logical that technology conquers those first. But as we saw with the example of the MP3 player, eliminating or drastically pushing one constraint usually only reveals another. Once most practical physical constraints are lifted, presenting the question *how* to do things, there is a completely new level of dilemmas and constraints. If there are no barriers to using technology in terms of time or money, the question moves to *whether* or *why* we should use certain technologies, or functionalities and possibilities offered by technology. Both the consequentialist and universalist would agree that those are worthwhile and more fundamental questions. They would just disagree on when to answer them. Consequentialists would judge the situation based on whether the outcome is good; universalists would like to determine that up front, based on the intention.

The new set of dilemmas, constraints or barriers for technology innovation are not technical but ethical in nature. What should we do with technology and what not? Or should we do everything technology allows us to do, as this is what evolution suggests? What knowledge should we have and what not? Should the freedom for research be restricted because of possible unethical consequences?

I stated it before already. You can't undo knowledge, an issue for the consequentialists, and you can't determine all intention up front, an issue for the universalists. The two instruments used most so far are regulation and transparency. Regulation is a top-down approach. Some types of research are (or have been) forbidden. Think, for instance, of stem cell research. Transparency is more of a peer-oriented mechanism. Research and research data should be public.[4] This is pretty well established in the exact sciences, but is not on the level where it should be in many of the social sciences.

But rules and procedures, as valuable and needed as they are, can only do so much. The forces of curiosity, innovation, progress and evolution seem to find ways around it. Nobel-prize winner Manfred Eigen suggests that the answer is not in trying to regulate and restrict knowledge, but in accumulating even more knowledge to harness all the knowledge we already have to get a grip on our future. He essentially proposes to use the forces of

---

4 Science has become too complex and interconnected to do alone anyway. James Bond type structures in deserted places where scientific teams work on devices to destruct the world, funded by a rich villain, are not possible.

progress themselves to control and steer them. In other words, the best way forward is even more forward.

But what additional knowledge do we need? Three areas come to mind: knowledge of the basics, usage feedback and contextual knowledge.

Understanding the Basics

In his 2008 article "Is Google Making Us Stupid?" in Atlantic Magazine, technology writer Nicholas Carr confesses his skill of deep reading is in danger. Is sitting down, reading an article, essay or book, really getting into the story, or trying to carefully follow a train of thought that is laid out middle-age mind rot? No, it's the Internet. As the mind continuously reprograms itself, a different style of reading leads to a different style of thinking. And the Web is structured around a much more fragmented style of reading – little nuggets of information, linked together in countless ways, and surrounded by advertisements. The Web seems to be built for distraction, hopping from one small bit to the next, instead of the focus that traditional book-reading invites the reader to have. Our reading strategies have changed from being effective, absorbing new knowledge into our own frame of mind, to being efficient, quickly finding what we are looking for. Is this different reading strategy a bad thing? Socrates, in the writings of Plato, argued that reading leads to rhetoric deficiency, compared to debating skills. In fact, I heard someone argue that if books would have been invented after video games, parents would have been worried because books don't allow you to interact and don't have the multi-sensory richness of games.

Regardless of whether Web reading is good or bad for our intelligence, it is good to have a choice – to be able to do proper deep reading on a subject, combined with quickly synthesizing information from various sources, representing multiple perspectives. Being a child of my time, I would suggest to learn deep-reading first before allowing technology to help you jump between sources quickly.

When we rely too heavily on technology and devices, we disengage from the world around us. You may argue that calculators allow us to focus on the logic of what we are trying to achieve, instead of losing ourselves in manual calculations. But where does the understanding of logic come from? Probably from being able to process arithmetic in our brains and with pen and paper as well.[5] Professional programmers benefit from having coded Java before starting with more advanced environments; Java teaches logic better. Accountants benefit from doing bookkeeping by hand before using financial packages. It allows them to predict the inner workings better. Car drivers should learn how to navigate without a system before relying on a TomTom or other GPS device.

Having basic skills in areas where we depend on technology allows us to survive in case the technology fails. Granted, there are practical limitations. Unless you are a boy scout, not many feel the urge to understand how to purify water or practice making fire without matches or a lighter. But in the Western world, confidence levels about the supply of water are higher than the confidence people have in IT. A second reason why having basic skills is good is that they help you understand whether systems and technologies deliver the right output –to see the result of a calculation on the calculator or a destination on the navigation system and think "that doesn't feel right." Where did the feeling come from? It is the result of having built a good frame of reference first.

Understanding Use

Even 25 years ago we had usability laboratories, where people could be observed using systems. This provided tremendously valuable input for the engineers design-

---

5 I hate spreadsheets; they invite messy structures and are very error prone. But if you need to build analytical skills, it doesn't harm to have to set up a decent spreadsheet or two before using more advanced statistical tools.

ing the "user experience." Within ambient computing, the user experience is either completely transparent (it is simply there and gets its input from invisible sensors) or manifests itself in many different ways, for instance on a range of devices depending on where you are and what you are doing, such as your tablet, smartphone, car or glasses. But essentially it is still driven by engineering thinking, where an optimized design is deciding how the system will look for the user. One-directional. But how does the user look like to the system? There's no telling. Systems should be more open to taking feedback regarding use and unanticipated use.

Many large websites are not truly designed anymore. Rather, screens are generated based on specific user input, and on the templates and content in the web content management system. I think we've all had the experience of being stuck or running around in circles, trying to find a way out. Web servers can record every click, and analytics can help interpret where users give up, but the input is not very rich. It is not possible to see how the user is reacting through facial expressions, hitting the keyboard and shouting at the system. What if we could make usability laboratories more scalable? Think of using Microsoft Kinect style technology, where an application can watch us and adapt.[6] It could suggest, for instance, what to do next based on the experience with other users. It could suggest the right help topics, or direct a user to a call center or web care team.

System design should also solicit unexpected feedback. Systems routinely offer users recommendations based on their preferences, customer segment and what other comparable users have done in the past. Although technically

---

6 Face recognition is being used for smartphones, replacing a password. I don't see any acceptance problems here. The question, of course, is if users feel comfortable being watched and analyzed while interacting with their phones, tablets and computers, and how to address these issues.

this leads to user preference feedback and creates a learning loop, these recommendations only reinforce the picture the system already had and lead to even more rigid recommendations the next time around. Different ways of suggesting the unexpected are needed, based on principles of serendipity – finding something useful you weren't specifically looking for. Systems should be more like a shop in which you can roam around and be inspired by everything that's there. Experiment with proximity of options and recommendations by systems, creating a virtual form of market basket analysis,[7] or systematically ask for feedback on random recommendations. These strategies are suboptimal in nature and counterintuitive to the engineering approach. Perhaps systems (and their designers) shouldn't try to be smarter all the time, trying to guess user preferences correctly.

Outliers are the first sign of change. Systems that do not recognize differences in use over time, or a different context in which they are used, run the risk of disconnecting from reality. Not good for systems we depend on.

Understanding the Context

Zen and the Art of Motorcycle Maintenance is the world's most read book on the philosophy of technology. The core of the message is a description of two extreme views on the use of technology. There are some who see technology, their motorcycle, as something they use. They know how to operate it, but feel they don't need to understand how it works. A technology is simply the sum of its parts; and if one part is broken, it needs to be fixed or replaced. That's what highly skilled and trained mechanics are for. They have the experience, do nothing else all day and have all the right tools. The other group sees the beauty of the technology itself. They see a larger picture of how parts interact with each other and are influenced by the con-

---

7 Market basket analysis tells you which items consumers typically buy together, like bread and butter, or trousers and socks.

text in which they operate. One part may be broken, but it might have been caused by something else that is not working properly. And if you are driving on your motorcycle, weather conditions partly determine how smoothly the engine runs. There is no mechanic traveling with you to make tiny adjustments. And if a paperclip helps as a tool to fix something, by all means it should be used.

Although the book focused more on the need to understand technology, and become one with it, it makes a small point that I think is worth emphasizing. It is not enough to understand the technology as a sum of all parts, and not even enough to understand the technology as a sum greater than all parts. As weather conditions affect the performance of the engine, you can induce a general rule. For a technology to be successful, it is particularly important to understand the context in which the technology is used. This idea is supported by the definition of "wisdom," which is the object of philosophy itself. Wisdom is not only understanding the matter at hand, but particularly the context in which it matters.[8]

For instance, let's take a look at decision support systems that help judges in determining the right sentence. For the acceptance of a system, it is very important that the rules that drive a sentence recommendation be transparent and that every recommendation can be traced back. In many cases, the process can be automated, and perhaps technically it is not required to route the sentence through an actual judge. It would make the process better (more objective), more cost-effective, and much faster. Cost, quality and speed, the three pillars of an efficient operation, are all served at the same time. However, for such a system to be successful, it is equally important to understand how people will accept a sentence from a machine. Will it cause people to resist and overflow the system with appeals? This would certainly negatively affect the business case. What additional measures would

---

8 Also see the "In Search of Wisdom" chapter.

be needed for people to buy into such a system?

If you build a recommendation engine for YouTube to predict what other video clips we'd like to see, we need to understand how the human mind jumps from one association to the other. How else would such a system be able to provide recommendations you wouldn't think of yourself, but you'd like anyway?

If you build a business intelligence (BI) system to help analyze complex strategic issues, it is not enough to understand the data structure and the statistical techniques used to come to analytical conclusions. BI systems are already far more efficient than any human brains, but for such a system to be effective, we also need to understand human decision making – how people absorb and process information, weigh different factors, collaborate with others and eventually reach a conclusion. This sounds logical, but most business intelligence system designs do not take this into account at all and focus exclusively on the technical side of data structure and analysis.

As a last example, let's consider the implementation of a business process management system. Most business cases focus on operational excellence. If this means taking repetitive work out of the hands of the users, there are no immediate ethical consequences of using the technology. However, if the business case involves administrative professionals having to follow rigid rules and procedures, enslaving them to the system, the business case may be financially sound, but fail on ethical grounds. Human beings are motivated by factors such as autonomy, mastery and purpose. Most humans want to be able to plan and perform their duties the way they see fit for themselves, making every day a learning experience and seeing their contribution to the organizational goals.

If the goal of technology, that we increasingly depend on, is to augment human capability, we should have a clear understanding of human capabilities and how they vary per person. This is the context we should be looking for.

Technology Realism

In the end, I am a technology optimist. I have to be. Technology is our evolutionary path, even as a species. Technology pessimism means there is no future, no perspective. I believe technological innovation should be encouraged, sponsored, and enabled with every means possible because it can bring so much good to humanity. We should know as much as we can about it, and then some, as Manfred Eigen suggests.

Exactly this, however, is a realistic concern. Unlike in the Age of Reason, most of us no longer believe we can think everything through. The rationality of human beings has clear boundaries. In our actions and in our decision making, we are driven by more primal needs. We simply do not have the capacity to think through the consequences of our actions because there are too many variables. We tend to be structurally overconfident in our own abilities. Every individual has his own frame of mind, and total perspective on a matter is rare, if not impossible.

Manfred Eigen argued for more knowledge. I interpret that in various ways, understanding the basics, understanding the use of systems and understanding the context. Perhaps the most important understanding of context is to realize that we don't know the consequences of technology innovation. Socrates got it right when he explained that the one reason he could think of why people called him wise was that at least he realized he didn't know, where others thought they knew.

In conclusion, there are no simple answers here (most likely not even complex answers). Partly we will simply learn by suffering the consequences, like the effect of nuclear weapons. Sometimes we will discover that something good can come out of it. Some will claim that nuclear energy is a good source of energy; however, after the Fukushima accident in Japan in 2011, that group has shrunk. Sometimes something bad will come out of inventions aimed for the good, like side effects of certain medications. This is what the consequentialists will propose as the way forward.

The universalists demand to know the rules up front. If we know that a certain cure can kill as well, we should keep searching for one that doesn't. If we can imagine a scenario that cars driven by computers instead of humans can lead to horrible accidents, we should first use technologies like this in more restricted environments to completely test them before selling them as a commercial product.

Both universalists and consequentialists will agree that the way forward is in public discourse. An open debate. Simply banning stem cell research is not the answer, but instructing scientists to organize open public debate as part of the research procedure can be. On a case-by-case basis as a community, we need to build an understanding – as much as we humanly can – about the role technology plays in our society. Sometimes we make mistakes, and we learn. Sometimes, when society is uncomfortable, we need to delay and continue the discussion, as much as the scientists want to continue (which I think is better than just saying "no," as the same research will pop up elsewhere anyway). And sometimes, we'll get it right. Form your opinion, voice it, and keep an open mind.

Read. Listen. Talk. Write.

Whose Data Is It, Anyway?

If you've done nothing wrong / You've got nothing to fear.
Everyone has their own number / In the system that we operate under.
To the whole project, it's brand new / Conceived solely to protect you.
We're moving to a situation / Where your lives exist as information.
-Pet Shop Boys, "Integral," 2007

A world without government is a pretty horrible prospect. In such a world, or what Thomas Hobbes (1588-1679) called a "state of nature," everyone would be at war in a struggle to survive. Life would be "nasty, brutal and short." To avoid such an environment, we prefer to hand over some of our natural rights to a government. We are willing to give up some of our freedom to receive protection. This is the purpose of government. Philosophers such as Hobbes and John Locke (1632-1704) have argued that creating a state is not a top-down exercise. A society is the result of a social contract between citizens. We accept the laws and customs of the country in which we live. We pay taxes and therefore receive protection, infrastructure and social benefits.

Trust
In the end, with all the checks and balances we have built in over the centuries, government as a system is based on trust. It has to be because it is too complex to fully control or even grasp. If we don't trust the system in which we live, we cannot trust anything anymore, simply because all people and institutions fall under the laws of their governments. If the system cannot be trusted, nothing within it can be trusted either. If the system cannot be trusted to do the right thing, it can only be assumed it will take out every element within the system that challenges the system. This would be a totalitarian state.

Yet, perhaps sometimes we trust the system a bit too much, particularly in situations where government has trouble keeping up with new developments such as technology advancements.

One example of a law having trouble keeping up with technology is the law against using mobile phones while driving. In many countries this is not restricted to actually talking on the phone –simply holding a phone in your hand while driving is forbidden. However, you are allowed to hold a navigation system or MP3 player in your hand. Herein is the confusion. For instance, an iPod Touch is difficult to distinguish from an iPhone. And what if the phone function of an iPhone is switched off and it is being used only as a navigation device or as an MP3 player?

We believe government will do the right thing, though. We expect the government to look after our best interests. After all, isn't that what government is supposed to do? Things will balance out eventually, we hope.

Big Brother is Watching You

Another area in which technology is moving faster than society's measures is data governance. The volume of data that is tracked about people on a daily basis is astonishing. On an average trip, your smartphone contains all the places you have been. You have been monitored by various surveillance cameras[1], such as at a stoplight or at the gas station. Most of your purchases are electronic. Some public transportation outlets no longer accept cash, and in some countries you can't even buy a train ticket – you have to use a chip card that is connected to your identity. Even parking fare creates a digital trace. Instead of simply buying a parking ticket, you need to enter your license plate number in the machine so that police can scan your license plate to see if you have paid. By the way, the purpose of your trip can be found online in your Google calendar, and you may have had email conversations about your trip. You can even be followed online through the data your navigation system sends to the server.

You may notice that not all of these examples include data collection by the authorities, such as your email, calendar and smartphone communication. However, police

---

1 Monitored by whom actually? Police? Private security firm? For what purposes? And optimized to track what behavior exactly?

are always allowed to access data and do so routinely. In the case of WikiLeaks, for instance, the authorities requested data from Twitter. Police can also ask for email traffic, phone records and all other electronic trails. Everything.

The more centralized the collected data, the easier it is to query. Of course, there are laws and rules about what data can be used for what purposes; but in practice this becomes a slippery slope. There is always function creep. Function creep means that the ways data is being used are being stretched and at some point are way beyond the purposes for which the data was collected. IT "best practices" make function creep an easily occurring phenomenon.

For instance, it is good practice to always store data at the lowest granular level. Even if you only need aggregated and anonymized data, it is better to store all atomic data in case different aggregations are needed later. An important architecture principle dictates that data models should be application-neutral, meaning they can be used for multiple purposes. In the Internet age, it is common to store as much data as possible in a single database to be accessed and used by various applications. In fact, reuse is a stated principle in the IT strategy of many authorities – re-use within the authority, between authorities and even between countries. Also, it turns out that privacy and security are not always the primary concerns. Ease of use and enabling the government tasks at hand are often the primary objectives.

This is concerning in multiple ways. If there are no natural barriers to query data, such as the effort or cost to access to certain databases, the reasons to indeed look up that data become more common as well. For instance, DNA is extracted from convicted criminals to test against old cases. Then perhaps – unrelated – DNA is extracted from newborns to test for various diseases. It does not take a stretch of the imagination to combine both processes to a new and "efficient" single process. Ethically unlikely today? Ethics and morals change over time, and sometimes much faster that one could imagine. Think of all the measures taken after 9/11.

Furthermore, it is very human to mix up all kinds of

causality issues. For instance, if burglars often wear black clothes, should we program the cameras in the street to keep an eye on everyone wearing black clothes? Ridiculous example? What about checking on young people driving expensive cars? This is a practice today in some places. Function creep simply happens. For instance, it is easy to quickly check everyone in the vicinity of a crime, based on their mobile phone location. Often, authorities simply send text messages asking assistance from witnesses. But if that data remains stored, it can easily be used to check if people repeatedly are in the neighborhood of crime scenes. Taxi drivers, the concierge of a hotel in a bad neighborhood, or perhaps family members of criminals become suspect quite soon. In general, without controls, it will become a routine operation to check everyone and everything.

Finally, we need to realize that although government's goal is to protect its citizens, it becomes an organism in its own right, with a will to sustain and survive. Not all decisions that authorities make are in the best interest of the people. Sometimes they are in the best interest of government itself. Data will also be used to monitor threats to government, and public transparency – allowing citizens to access data – has its limits.

TomTom

In the spring of 2011, European newspapers reported that police used TomTom navigation data for planning speed traps. There was a public outcry, and TomTom immediately responded by stopping these practices. But how did this happen?

One of TomTom's innovative services is to make the navigation devices bidirectional. It collects driver data in real-time, and it uses that data and the data of all other subscribers to notify drivers of traffic jams more reliably than through the radio – even traffic on smaller roads. To maximize the profit of this service and to price the service competitively, TomTom has stated in its terms and conditions that it is allowed to sell the collected data in an aggregated and anonymized manner.

The infrastructural authorities in charge of the roads found good use for the data. It helps them see where road improvements are needed to eliminate recurring traffic jams or, vice versa, analyzing the data on how to minimize the traffic jams caused by current roadwork. So far, no problem. However, at some point, the same data set landed in the hands of the police, who used it to calculate average speeds and plan speed traps. Somehow this hit the newspapers.

So here is the question: Is the use of this TomTom data set appropriate or not? What is the first reaction you have after reading this case? "No way!" or "Sure... so what?" Actually, it can be argued both ways.

For instance, the data is anonymous, aggregated, and legally bought. Citizens do not have to give consent for the police to use the data, just as the police don't need consent to flash cars that are speeding. Furthermore, the data wasn't used for fining people after the fact – it was used to set up speed traps to catch people at the actual moment of speeding. In fact, this type of data-based decision making is an example of more efficient use of taxpayers' money. It replaces a more elaborate process of physically searching for places where drivers tend to speed. Furthermore, as a society, we have laws and they should be enforced. The consequence of speeding is a fine. And enforcing speed limits is in the best interest of society and its citizens. It improves safety on the road, and less speeding means less carbon dioxide emissions.

And finally, why can't the police use technology to improve the effectiveness and efficiency of speed traps if we, the citizens, can use technologies such as Twitter to avoid speed traps or even use the cameras in our smart phones to film police brutality[2]? Consumer technology

---

2 Granted, in this technology rat race between citizens and government, government has the unique advantage of being able to ban the use of technologies, such as laser gun jammers.

has created a situation in which we can watch our governments as much as they can watch us.

Yet, TomTom's immediate reaction was to stop these practices. It felt that the police using its data was bad for business. Customers didn't sign up for that. They pay extra for added value services such as dynamic traffic jam monitoring. Customers create the value by supplying data individually to benefit from the data collectively. They are supposed to benefit from supplying the data, not be punished with it. And this feels like a slippery slope of data use already. What's next? Direct use of atomic data that was tracked anyway, because – from an engineering perspective – this is a more flexible way to collect data? This is not an outrageous thought. Google was reprimanded for collecting router data from people's homes when scanning streets for its Streetview service. Why would government be better?

Another reason for the public outcry regarding TomTom may not have been about the actual use of data, but about how the police got to the data. They didn't approach TomTom directly, but reused data that was purchased for a different purpose. This example may simply be "yet another" example of "what is wrong with the police." The police already have a bad reputation for writing speeding and parking tickets more for funding purposes than for law enforcement itself. And why don't they focus more on burglars and other "real" criminals?

As you can see, both lines of argumentation can be defended. What is your final opinion, for or against? I find this hard to answer. I can see both sides equally, but in different roles. As a citizen I would argue for, but as a TomTom customer I think I would argue against. And do I have to be either for or against? All I can honestly say is that given the active discussion in the newspapers regarding this issue, the discussion on data governance is clearly not closed.

Who Owns Your Data?

So far most of the examples I used came from the public sector, such as the police. But the same issues arise in the private sector. Digital data governance, as a relatively new phenomenon, isn't clearly organized. Who owns the location-based data on your smartphone? The phone company? The phone manufacturer? Or do you feel you own the text messages, voicemail, emails and pictures you stored on your phone? And who owns the status updates you put on Facebook? You or Facebook, for advertising and profiling purposes?

It doesn't seem to bother most of us much, but would you feel equally comfortable learning that the telephone company transcribes your telephone conversations and sells them to advertisers? In a sense, this is happening already. Various phone companies have used, or are using, "deep pocket inspection" to monitor which applications you use on your smartphone because applications such as WhatsApp and Skype pose a threat to their revenue. The questions go on and on, including: Who owns the data TomTom and Google Street View collect about your travel routes? An old-world, personal example is: do I own the intellectual property of my books, or does the publisher since the book is a physical product?

Sure, all of this is carefully taken care of in the small print of the terms and conditions of the services we use, but – given the public discussions taking place when users find out what happens with "their" data – do the terms and conditions reflect what we feel is fair?

So, the most obvious question in the debate on data governance is about ownership. If you create data, who does it belong to? It sounds funny to ask "who owns your data," but that contradiction is exactly the issue. Which data belongs to you, and which data is just about you? And what data would we be talking about?

Who owns your contact details? It falls pretty naturally under the social contract to allow the authorities to have the primary storage of your address, nationality and other personal information about your identity and whereabouts. I don't think many people would find this a serious issue.

But what about medical data? It would be advantageous

for many if there were such a thing as a national (or even universal) electronic medical file, accessible by healthcare providers, to make sure there is a holistic picture of the health of a patient. This would prevent many unnecessary deaths during emergencies and unnecessary errors by multiple specialists administering harmful combinations of medication. Obviously the structure would be centrally governed to enforce a storage and retrieval standard, but many would agree the data should be minimally owned by the patient, in the sense that the patient controls who can access the data.

What about our financial data? Who owns the transaction data, the balance on our accounts, and the overview of our shares portfolio? Do we own that data or does the bank? I reckon most people do not have a problem with the bank owning that information. Yet both are very privacy-sensitive. Perhaps the difference between medical data and financial data is that in the case of medical data, there are many different stakeholders, and it can be in the best interest of the customer (patient) to share the data. In the case of financial data, the information is between the bank and you (with the exception of some authorities, such as the tax office). So it seems that in some cases we care more than in other cases.

There are also many subjects that are less sensitive, yet still very personal. Think of hobbies, musical taste, your favorite authors, food preferences and other information that you regularly leave behind on websites to get access to certain services. This is the information that is used for targeting specific information (and advertisements) to you. Who owns this information? Or to restate this in a more practical form: Would you like to be in control over who sees this information and what is being done with it?

Perhaps an even more fundamental question is: How important is having ownership of data we generate? We generate things all the time for which we don't take responsibility and ownership, e.g., carbon dioxide emissions. Economists call this "external effects". What is the difference? Carbon emissions don't really have semantics, they are not personal and don't describe aspects of our lives or our actions. The only thing you could theoretically do with carbon emissions is to trace it back to who generated it. And even this is not likely. But data is much more sensitive. As the Pet Shop Boys sang, "We're moving to a situation / where your lives exist as information."

Principles of Liberalism – Freedom and Control

Given all the questions here and – admittedly – the lack of clear answers, governance in the world of digital data is partly, or even largely, uncharted territory. However, the discussion of ownership has been going on for centuries in the physical world, e.g., land ownership.

John Locke argued mankind has natural rights, consisting of life, liberty and property. An English philosopher and physician, Locke is considered the father of liberalism, and he was an inspiration to the founding fathers of the United States. His words are in the American Declaration of Independence almost verbatim. Life, liberty and the property of all are unalienable rights that even the government cannot take away. In fact, the whole point of government is to protect these rights.

Let's briefly zoom in on the natural right of property of all. According to Locke, what gives us the right to have property is related to the labor we put into it. If we see unowned land, putting a fence around it is not enough to establish ownership. However, under liberal principles, we own our labor, so once we put labor into developing that land (e.g., for agricultural purposes), we own that land. You can argue the same way with data. If you, as a civilian, create data, this is labor; thus you own the data you have created.

At the same time, Locke argues the need for a social contract in which we give up some rights in exchange for protection from anarchy. Government needs to be paid, which is done through taxes. The income that pays for the taxes is the fruit of our labor, yet government also demands its share. Liberty and freedom have limits as well, namely the borders of where we affect the liberty and freedom of others. To prevent others from doing you harm, so must you be prevented from harming others. This is a liberal principle that applies on a personal level, but also between nations.

Locke introduces a continuous tension – dynamic – between two principles: owning the fruit of our labor (property) and the borders of liberty. The balance between the two shifts over time, based on changes in political beliefs, morality, power and safety[3].

In the current climate, the balance is clearly biased toward government and control, limiting our personal freedom. We give our governments more consent. In a worldwide war against terrorism, identity information is widely shared between governments. Think, for instance, of the European Union sharing flight passenger data with the United States. However, there are still limits. For further anti-terrorism measures, the U.S. also asked the EU for banking data of its citizens, which was not supplied.

Even on a personal level, we ask the authorities to take control. We think that having cameras everywhere improves our safety. Not only do we accept cameras in the street, we actively lobby for cameras in more places, such as child day care centers and schools. Parents frequently lobby for cameras in the schoolyards, and even children see this as a more effective measure against bullying than peer social control. There is a popular smartphone application that, based on your current location, plots the addresses of local sex offenders on the map, including pictures of that person, but without context. We expect – we demand – for this data to be public. We can even track the location of our children via smartphone applications. It begs the question: To what extent we are allowed to track what our children do? We need to protect them, but they have a right to privacy too.

---

3 This is exactly the reason why the popular opinion of "If you've got nothing to hide, you've got nothing to fear" is so naive.

How did we manage before smartphones? Is having a constant dialogue with our children –building mutual trust – not sufficient anymore? What seems to have happened is that we have externalized the notion of responsibility. "Who is responsible for all this?" is the first question that comes up when something goes wrong. Society has become so complex that we don't feel we have enough control to take responsibility over our environment ourselves. Will this trend continue, or will reverse at some point? Time will tell.

Organizing Data Governance - And Many Ways to Mess it Up Again

Whether the balance is more toward the authorities or the balance sways more to personal freedom, the question of how to organize governance always remains. And any change in the balance between freedom and control has its impact on the organizational aspects of governance. Perhaps there are parallels between commercial enterprises and the public sector.

Organizing data governance within a company in a decentralized way has proven to be difficult. It often leads to many – and unnecessary – versions of the truth, a fragmentation of definitions and minimal standards on how to define and govern definitions and data. As a result, organizations with decentralized data governance can only analyze data with a limited scope and can't optimize their complete value chain. The best result you can get is partial optimization and therefore suboptimal results.

Yet, the opposite – centralized data governance – also doesn't work. Perhaps there is a single version of the truth, a single technology to work with and a clear standard on how to define terms, but are the outcomes still relevant for the various lines of business? It seems that centralized data governance leads to consistent group reporting, such as financial consolidation, but business units have a reason for being: They offer a unique contribution. Somehow this uniqueness needs to be reflected in the way it collects data about the business.

The solution that businesses have found so far is to govern by committee. Information managers from multiple business units confer and set standards and priorities. Within those standards business units can define their own data needs and, where possible, can consolidate into a single structure or definition.

Perhaps this is the answer to the question of who governs government. Some believe that government has so many stakeholders and that, as government becomes a goal in its own right, data may easily be (ab)used for purposes not intended by the initial data collection. Perhaps the complexity of government can work for governance purposes too. Data governance could be a distributed principle. The structure of data may very well be centralized – there are many advantages to having a standard way of storing and defining the data. But that doesn't mean the data has to be stored centrally. As citizens, we have seen many examples of how security can be compromised and personal data becomes available in places it shouldn't. Within a distributed mechanism it doesn't really matter which particular authority stores the data, or if the data is stored in a citizen-owned environment. The centralized standard is a hub that simply routes requests to the right storage.

There is a subtle but crucial difference between a distributed mechanism structured by a central hub and a fragmented mechanism. In a fragmented mechanism, all kinds of data are stored in many different places. Systems replicate data to many other systems through point-to-point interfaces. A severely underestimated issue is that of identity theft. If someone uses another person's identity and the authorities respond to the wrong person, there's almost no stopping the machine. The responding authority may quickly discover they're looking at the wrong person, but by then their data has been copied to multiple other databases. Even worse, as advanced interfaces keep systems "in sync," corrections are replaced by the previous error automatically, and all the time. Once a mistake has been made, it is almost impossible to wipe it from fragmented and connected systems, leading to issues with almost every authority that has integrated its data. There are many recorded cases on how data mistakes haunt people for years.

In a distributed mechanism, data passes the hub. Requests and changes are logged, and the right authorizations can be given before data is used. One could even impose the idea of an expiration date on data. After the expiration it is wiped from decentralized systems and needs to be requested again via the hub.

It is still possible for authorities to use data for unintended purposes, but to do this on a grand scale would require the assistance of multiple authorities, which is not likely in a modern democracy.

Although the data modeling challenges alone are formidable, it seems like a good synthesis between the advantages of centralized and decentralized data governance. But what about all the consumer preference data we routinely leave behind on commercial websites and with commercial enterprises? Can we use the same principles? Microsoft has already experimented with something called Passport (later called Windows Live ID) that allowed you to log on once and then continue working with every subscribing website. Google has created a single log-on as well for its services. Perhaps the idea can be expanded to an electronic structure that is all encompassing and not only arranges a single sign-on, but also contains our advertising preferences and a module for rule-based authorizations in which you can opt in and opt out for various services. It would have to be persona-based, not person-based, so that we can create multiple profiles to reflect the various roles we would like to have online. Would you leave this to Google, Microsoft or Facebook?

Any competitive environment should foster innovation and lead to cost-efficient operations. But a commercial enterprise responds to its shareholders, not to its customers. And to differentiate from the competition, with giants such as Google and Microsoft, it is unlikely there will be standards, which leads to vendor lock-in.

The communitarian philosophers would probably point out a third way, a concept that has been proven to be extremely robust in financial services: the Raiffeisen concept. Communitarians, as a contemporary philosophical school of thought, believe in peer social control. Solutions to problems should be found through public debate, not by imposing top-down controls. Communitarians value the power of community, the ability of people to solve social and political issues in a self-organized manner. Safety comes from knitting a tight society in which people feel responsible for each other, instead of relying on school, social services and government in general. The Raiffeisen concept fits into the communitarian school of thought. Friedrich Wilhelm Raiffeisen (1818-1888) was a German mayor. Seeing farmers suffer at the hands of loan sharks, he came up with the idea of cooperative banking, a credit union owned by the farmers. The Raiffeisen concept is the most pure implementation of an insurance business model: creating a community of people who each contribute a little to help out those who need it. Some of the banks founded on Raiffeisen principles now belong to the larger and most trusted (!) banks in the world.

So, instead of leaving your consumer preference file with a commercial enterprise, it could be managed by a cooperative business owned by the users and operated by appointed management to govern standards and security. Perhaps it could be built based on open source standards, but not necessarily for free. The cooperative would own the framework and process requests, and the members would own their data and authorize the use of the data for various purposes. There are already some banks that expanded their services from financial products to data governance as a foothold in the entire electronic marketplace. However, it would be better off as a cooperative consortium, so that a single organization doesn't dominate the initiative. That would lead to the same lock-in problems that need to be avoided.

F* the System

Every complex system needs to be based on trust. Given the growing impact of data governance and the grave consequences of failing to organize it, the authorities will get it right eventually. Businesses exploiting their customers by the lack of good governance will ultimately adapt or fold.

What can we do in the meantime to test the trustworthiness of data governance or block its negative consequences? Years ago I heard of one university professor who used different middle initials every time he had to supply his name. This allowed him to track data sales over the years, mapping the provided initials with the mail he received from various companies. This is something everyone can do. In fact, it would be easy to organize an electronic community to share these patterns and build up a commercial data map. To avoid being profiled, you could swap bonus cards with your neighbor in the supermarket line, swap SIM cards with different mobile phones in the household (to confuse location tracking), or even better – someone should write an app that masks location, similar to anonymous remailers. Or someone should write an app that does the opposite – creates location data that tells the system you are many different place at the same time.[4] One well-known trick to avoid emails being tracked is to save them on the server as a "draft", and have the receiver open them with the same password the sender uses to log on. This way the email is never really sent.

In the meantime, perhaps we can also rely on the court jesters that every healthy governing system has – those who are brave enough to tell the truth to those in power. These would be the white hackers and whistleblowers who uncover security issues, dysfunctional policies and unintended use of data – our own data, created as the fruit of our own labor.

Until we get it right, eventually.

---

4 I wonder if apps like this will be accepted in the app stores of smartphone vendors.

Aristotelian
Architecture

Never trust a discipline that is not able to predict its own demise.

It seems that every system integrator, consultancy and analyst house has its own "maturity model." They help organizations measure how far along they are in certain disciplines, such as in systems administration, security, content management, integration and so forth. These models typically start with a stage called *ad hoc* or *reactive*, then go through stages such as *departmental* then almost invariably there is a stage indicating some kind of *integration*, and finally the situation is *optimized*.

There is No Such Thing as "Optimized"

The appeal of these models is easy to spot. Wouldn't we all want to be in the optimized stage? And if there are consultants who can help us spot where we are, where we want to be, and plot how we get there, isn't this the groundwork for any good strategy? Still, I think these models simply miss the mark. I don't think that at one moment you can say that you're done, that you have reached a state of being a high-performance organization, or being optimized in any way. I don't believe that there is any steady state, for that matter. Progress comes with ebbs and flows. At most moments in time, you will reach some kind of equilibrium, where the system, process, program or whatever supports what it needs to support. Then something changes again, disturbing the equilibrium. Technology moves on, user requirements progress, competitors raise the bar, customer demands shift, economic circumstances change, the regulatory environment tightens, and so forth. The list of potential changes is endless. These changes disrupt the current balance, and then you try to create a new equilibrium. Sometimes this is an improvement, and sometimes it is a step back, like with many things in life.[1] And if we must think in stages, where are the stages of decay and death? Technologies get absorbed into other ones, and some user requirements simply disappear. When was the last time you sent a fax?

In short, everything you don't put energy into decays – buildings, living creatures, friendships, relationships, systems, processes, everything. If you keep putting effort in, there may be improvement along the way, but you're never done. There is no such thing as optimized. Every manager knows that if you move your attention to one area, another area suffers. To use a metaphor, there is always one more plate turning than you can manage.

There is an underlying law of nature called *entropy*. Everything in nature flows from a concentrated form into some kind of disorder. In fact, entropy is a force of evolution. Evolution is based on a number of principles. First, there needs to be genetic variation. Every plant or animal, although belonging to a species, needs to be slightly different. Otherwise, there is no competitive advantage. Then, it needs to be possible to create new random permutations, based on inheritance. Lastly, there needs to be a competitive natural environment, in which only the most adaptive survive and in which the random permutations that do not have an environmental fit die. In a way, entropy drives change in nature and, at the same time, allows random permutations to occur.

Evolution and Enterprise Architecture

Evolution and enterprise architecture are very much related. From a cynical point of view, you could say that the forces of evolution have shaped most enterprise architectures. To quote one famous analyst[2]: "Most of you have an accidental architecture. I mean, I can only hope you didn't deliberately design what you have in place."

---

1 When you create a model that contains an optimized end state, you live within the paradigm of that model, and you are not able to look beyond the borders of it. This is exactly like examining our own lives. As human beings, we are not able to look beyond our own deaths and need to accept existing only within our own paradigm of life. However, if you are able to look beyond the borders of your own discipline, you master it and are potentially able to also grasp a new paradigm.
2 Andy Kyte, Gartner Fellow, Gartner Symposium/ITxpo, 2010, France

Enterprise architecture (EA) can formally be defined as "a rigorous description of the structure of an enterprise, which comprises enterprise components (business entities), the externally visible properties of those components, and the relationships (e.g., the behavior) between them. EA describes the terminology, the composition of enterprise components, and their relationships with the external environment, and the guiding principles for the requirement (analysis), design, and evolution of an enterprise. This description is comprehensive, including enterprise goals, business process, roles, organizational structures, organizational behaviors, business information, software applications and computer systems."

This definition already contains the word *evolution*. When we focus on that, we can define enterprise architecture as all activities to counter the forces of entropy and keep our enterprise focused and composed. Enterprise architecture maintains order and battles the decay and chaos that entropy causes. This means an enterprise architecture needs to be resilient to resist entropy. In many cases, this is done by building a rigorous and robust enterprise architecture that will stand the test of time. Obviously, an enterprise architecture is a reference model. It takes time to get there, and practicalities under way may force you to make decisions that are not supported by the enterprise architecture. For instance, certain business applications may have their own workflow or content management, or come with their own reporting tools. But the goal of the enterprise architecture is to come as close as possible to an ideal state. Again, like with maturity models, we think in states.

Aristotle has the Answer

This thinking in states is deeply rooted in Western philosophy. Parmenides (5th century BC), a Greek philosopher predating Plato, felt that any motion and change in nature were nothing more than manifestations of an unchanging reality. In reality, everything "is." If something changes, it needs to move from what it is to something else that "is." In between, change would mean a mix between "to be" and "to not be." Impossible, according to Parmenides. Plato continued on this path. Real knowledge about objects in this world is universal too, and doesn't change. Plato felt the process of such objects *becoming* was not accessible to human beings. The idea of the underlying truth of being has dominated Western philosophy ever since. Heraclitus (535 – 475 BC) took a different approach. He is most famous for his words "panta rhei, kai ouden menei," meaning "everything flows, and nothing remains still."[3] Heraclitus didn't think in states, but rather much more in terms of continuous movement. Unfortunately, the work of Heraclitus has been less influential.

Aristotle (384–322 BC) argues that we can also observe all the changes in the world around us. Aristotle starts, like Plato and Parmenides, by pointing out that the most important characteristic of any object is its existence. But change and movement – in other words the becoming of the object – is a transition from its potential to be to the act of being, with a certain degree of perfection. This transition has a certain internal or external cause. In short, Aristotle suggests for each change or movement, we should ask four questions. What did change? What caused that change? What is the result of the change? What is the purpose of the change?

To answer these questions, Aristotle identified four "causes." Causes are best translated as "explanatory conditions and factors." The four causes are the material cause (causa materialis), the efficient cause (causa efficiens), the formal cause (causa formalis) and the final cause (causa finalis).

It turns out that these causes are a very useful framework for a resilient enterprise architecture. Not resilient in terms of being robust, but built in terms of cause and effect. Not based on an ideal state that is to be pursued, but built on the assumption of continuous change and movement.

---

3 It is not recorded that Heraclitus spoke or wrote those words, but they were attributed to him later to describe his philosophy.

The Four Causes

Aristotle was not the first to ask the question "why" in trying to understand the world. In fact, "why" is one of the most important philosophical questions one can ask. Others before Aristotle had explored the "why" of things. Although, according to Aristotle, others had come up with all elements of causality that Aristotle mentioned but Aristotle was the first to describe the four causes as a comprehensive theory.

The term that Aristotle used was *aition*, which is "an explanation for how something came to be." This is a wider term than the English term "cause," which comes the closest. Today "cause" is very much connected to "effect," through cause-and-effect relationships. If we increase prices by x%, sales will go down by y%. If we bump our head, we get a bruise. If we leave the steak on the barbeque too long, it will burn. This is what Aristotle would call the efficient cause, but there are other causes as well.

The four causes are usually explained with the example of a statue. The material cause of the statue is marble, the material of which the statue is made. The efficient cause is the sculptor and his chisel, how the statue was made. The formal cause consists of what the statue portrays, for instance a woman. The final cause describes the purpose of the statue, such as depicting love or, more mundane, highlighting the center of a square.

Or take the example of mankind itself. A human being is made of flesh and bones, which constitutes the material cause. It is produced by its father and mother, which is the efficient cause. A human being is recognizable by its features. We all have legs and arms, a nose and the ability to reason, which is the formal cause. For what purpose, the final cause, is a question that has many different answers, ranging from simply sustaining the species (biological) to fulfilling your full potential (humanistic) to living a life worthy of deserving a place in heaven (religious).

Finally, let's take another example, a little closer to enterprise architecture, by asking "Why did the house collapse?" The material cause might be the quality of the stones that were used. The efficient cause is that the builders didn't do a good job using the materials or that bad weather caused the collapse. The formal cause might be the blueprint that contained errors. The final cause in this example is that cost was preferred over quality.

In all examples, multiple causes can play a role in the explanation of an object or an event. Leaving out one cause, or choosing a different explanation as a result of one of the four causes, would lead to different results.

Material Cause

There has to be an unmoved mover, the thing that comes first. In Aristotle's view, what we can assume to be present are the materials of which the object is composed. We can define this broadly and refer to bronze as the raw material of a statue, or define multiple levels of material causes, where the bronze is caused by its elements, ultimately leading to the atomic level of the material. The statue is caused by its raw materials because without the bronze it wouldn't be there. As Aristotle tries to describe change through his four causes, the raw material undergoes change as well. For instance, the bronze needs to be melted and molded to become part of the statue. The material cause is not limited to a single type of material. The material cause of the house, in the example I used, includes concrete, wood, glass and spikes (notice that a spike in itself has four causes as well – it consists of material, it was produced, it has a form, and a meaning). Materials can cause certain things, but others not. Bronze is only suitable for a certain type of statue; from the point of view of the other causes, another statue might benefit more from marble.

The link with enterprise architecture is pretty obvious. The material cause describes the technology level. All technologies in use by the organization together form the material cause. This includes business technologies such as content management and business intelligence; hardcore technologies such as development environments and integration tools; and supporting technologies taking care of systems management, security and so forth. If you lack certain technologies, it is not possible to create enterprise architectures that deem those technologies necessary. Some organizations may be able to invest in their own technologies, but for most organizations the technologies available are indeed the unmoved mover. They are assumed to be there.

Yet, it is not that simple. Others would argue that technologies are not the cause of an architecture. They are the effect. One would choose the technologies needed to compile a certain enterprise architecture. Still, they are the material cause, as Aristotle defined "cause" in a broader sense. The technologies, chosen or already available, form a description of the enterprise architecture envisioned or in place. Furthermore, enterprise architects work within certain paradigms as well. It is hard to include technologies you are not aware of. In strategy, this debate was summarized as "strategy follows structure," or "structure follows strategy." The only conclusion that remains in such a heated debate is that both are interdependent. New strategies come out of existing structures, and new structures are the result of new strategies. The relationship between enterprise architecture and technologies is the same.

I also include skills and organizational capabilities in the material cause. This seems to be in contradiction to Aristotle. He regarded the sculptor and his skills as the efficient cause. However, there is an important difference. In the case of a statue, the sculptor is external to the statue; he creates it. In the case of organizational capabilities, they are part of the enterprise architecture itself and therefore part of the material cause. Obviously, it is not enough to own technologies. It is equally important to master them or to know where to get the right skills. Another essential organizational capability in an adaptive enterprise architecture is being able to spot new and innovative technologies, and use them in a meaningful way. Consequently, organizations need to be able to absorb those new technologies into the architecture, as part of absorbing all external and internal change to existing systems and processes.

Efficient Cause

The efficient cause comes closest to what we today would call cause-and-effect. The bad weather causes the house to be flooded or the sculptor with his chisel creates a statue. To be more precise, according to Aristotle, it is the knowledge and the skills of the sculptor that form the efficient cause, the art of sculpting in general. The efficient cause is the primary source of change.

This cause is different from what I have seen in other enterprise architecture frameworks. Most framework take a closed-system approach, describing only the elements within the frameworks, all other things being equal. If the primary source of change is the efficient cause, then the external factors that shape and reshape the organization deserve quite some attention. Understanding the efficient cause of enterprise architecture can be accomplished through a stakeholder analysis. A very useful framework to do this is the Performance Prism that was developed at Cranfield University in the UK. This framework defines both stakeholder contributions and requirements. Stakeholders include customers, suppliers, employees, investors, authorities and society at large.

Stakeholders each have contributions. As a stakeholder, they have an interest in the success of the organization. By offering their business, opinions and trust, customers fuel the organization's growth. In addition to good products and services, suppliers should offer an efficient buying process that is reliable, fast, easy and leads to the right price. Employees offer their hands, their minds, their hearts and their voices in the market. Investors offer capital and their support, but also take credit risk. Authorities ensure there is a fair market, with clear rules, and can provide advice. Lastly, the community provides an infrastructure within which to do business. This includes access to skills and the means to create positive public relations through the media.

An enterprise architecture describes the impact of these contributions on the organizational structure, its systems and processes; and it describes how changing contributions affect the enterprise architecture. But there is more. In order to count on stakeholder contributions, we need to take stakeholder requirements into account as well.

Customers require what you demand from your suppliers. Next to good products and services, you should offer an efficient buying process that is reliable, fast, easy and leads to the right price. Suppliers require what you have to offer as a customer: profit, growth, your opinion and trust. Employees require pay and care, but also the opportunity to build skills and receive feedback on how their work is contributing to organizational success. Investors obviously expect a return, but also transparency so they can keep faith in their investment. Authorities expect organizations to obey the law, conduct business in a fair way, run safe operations and be truthful in their reporting. The community is looking for jobs, a share of the wealth that is created and a certain amount of fidelity.

As the Performance Prism describes these stakeholder contributions and requirements in great detail, the change that they bring can be detected, to a certain extent predicted, and taken into account to build an agile enterprise architecture. It is important to remember that relationships with the environment are reciprocal. Simply extracting value from the larger ecosystem is not sustainable.

Formal Cause

The formal cause describes how the object of analysis looks – its form. A statue can depict a human being, a horse, or an abstract three-dimensional pattern called "happiness." Understanding an object's form is needed to describe that particular object. In order for something to be called a house, it usually has a roof, a door, windows and, in some houses, a chimney and a garden. Without this explanation and a clear blueprint, the house could look totally different or – in the absence of any formal cause – be just a collection of materials neatly packed on a piece of land.

With the knowledge we have today, the formal cause doesn't have to be a static result, like a statue, a house or – in terms of an enterprise architecture – a description of all the organizational functions the architecture supports.

With the advent of service-oriented architectures, we can take the formal cause one step further and create an agile enterprise architecture that is continuously being recomposed. Service-oriented architecture may form the technology component, but the thinking behind it can also be applied to organizations, creating a service-oriented organization. If all activities are seen as a business service, not as a step in a process, they can be put together in multiple, probably countless, ways. A business service is a unit of work that leads to a transferable result: The result is sufficient for the next person to continue, even if the next person is the customer. Viewed from the IT perspective, a business service represents the functionality to be developed to support the task. From the perspective of the organization model, a business service represents the role an employee performs to complete the task. Business services are not focused on specific processes and products, but focused on competencies that can be used for a multitude of things. There are many business examples available. Since the beginning, breweries have realized that their distilling process can be used for other spirits as well, such as whisky. Amazon realized its infrastructure is not only capable of selling books, but also of selling second-hand books, goods other than books, and even IT capacity itself (cloud computing). Utility companies, such as the electricity company, sometimes offer invoicing services for other utilities, such as water and gas. The capability is at the center, not the product.[4]

---

4 Much of the description of what I call "business services" is based on the work I did with Emiel van Bockel around his concept of business elements.

If you think this through, this approach actually reconciles the opposing forces of entropy and evolution on one hand and enterprise architecture on the other. Enterprise architecture is no longer fighting evolution and entropy, but rather embraces it. In fact, service orientation on any level is very much like evolution. In order for biological components to mix, they need extreme standardization on the DNA level too. Random variation is nothing other than trying all kinds of DNA combinations.

It should be said that you can argue whether evolution belongs in the formal cause. Evolution creates random variation and doesn't concern itself with how something should look. And evolution certainly doesn't seem to belong in the final cause, as there is no meaning to random variation. Aren't the latter two causes more the territory of "intelligent design"? This argument is relatively easy to counter. Adaptation exists by the grace of evolution, and the form that fits its natural environment best will succeed and procreate.

Final Cause

The final cause is the most important. It describes the purpose of the object, the essence of its being. Once a final cause is in place, the material cause, efficient cause and formal cause can, in principle, be derived. They follow from the goal. If the final cause of a statue is to show the magnificence of the emperor going to battle on his horse, the first step is to make a wax model. Then the bronze is melted, poured, and further treated. Each and every step is bringing the idea of the statue closer to becoming reality.

At first, it is a bit odd that the final cause is a cause. Isn't it the result? The final effect? Aristotle maybe called the final cause the most important one because it is the initial idea that triggered the other causes. Because you wanted it to be reality, it becomes reality. Because you want to be an entrepreneur, you start your own business.

Still, the causality isn't that simple. Let's return for a second to the "structure follows strategy" debate. You may want to be the world's best basketball player; but if you are not tall and athletic, it is unlikely it is going to happen. And if you don't have an athletic posture, you probably would never have the idea to become the world's best basketball player. The final cause closes the loop. It is what triggers change, and it is the result of change.

One of the best books I read on the subject, *Enterprise Architecture as Strategy*, by Jeanne Ross, Peter Weill and David Robertson, elaborates greatly on different business operating models (different final causes) and how that leads to different enterprise architectures. Ross et al describe a two-by-two matrix, with one axis describing an increasing integration of business processes and the other describing increased business process standardization. Low standardization and low integration mean a diversified business strategy and operating model. The key capability for any enterprise architecture is to provide economies of scale, without limiting independence.

A high level of standardization with low integration is the main characteristic of a business model based on replication. Business units share best practices, and the enterprise architecture focuses on creating, managing and disseminating standard components.

A high level of integration with a low level of standardization is the hallmark of a coordinated business, where various specialized business units need to collaborate. Enterprise architecture in this model is all about providing access to shared data and data exchange. Highly integrated and standardized businesses benefit most from an enterprise architecture that reinforces standard processes and enterprise systems.

Depending on the operating model you have, a certain enterprise architecture will follow. The final cause. Yet, new technologies and more agile enterprise architectures also enable new blends in operating models, and once in a while completely new business models. The final effect.

The Ultimate Enterprise Architecture Framework?

Aristotle aimed to explain all form and matter with his four causes. This includes enterprise architecture, even though obviously the concept didn't exist in Aristotle's time. Does this mean that the four causes are the ultimate enterprise architecture framework? Probably not. Existing leading frameworks such as Zachman and TOGAF are generic frameworks to cover all sorts of enterprise architectures, while at the same time being very specific in covering aspects of enterprise architecture only. They are not theories-of-everything. This makes existing enterprise architecture frameworks particularly valuable.

In fact, the Zachman Framework is almost structured in terms of causes. It introduces a number of levels (contextual, conceptual, logical, physical and detailed) and then introduces a series of questions for each level. These questions are: Why? How? What? Who? Where? When? This is a very structured approach toward creating a detailed explanation, very much like Aristotle's causes but practically applied and offering much more guidance specifically toward creating an enterprise architecture.

Still, there is always room for improvement, even when the advice is 2500 years old. For instance, it took TOGAF until version 9 to become more business focused, and therewith introduce what we here call the final cause. Before version 9, TOGAF was really IT focused, architecture for its own sake. And although Zachman offers a comprehensive framework, it could do better in emphasizing the efficient cause. The "who" question is still very much about the material cause, identifying the roles and skills within the organization. The same goes for the stakeholders that are connected to the various levels in the framework – largely internal to the business. The contextual level could (should?) develop more into the direction of the efficient cause.

One thing is certain: Enterprise architecture and philosophy are very much related. One of the oldest fascinations in philosophy is about what defines beauty. Aesthetics. A fascination that most enterprise architects will share.

The Myth of the
One Version of
the Truth

When Confucius was asked what he would do first if he were in power, he responded: "Cleanse the definitions of terms we use!"

According to Confucius, nothing is so destructive for peace, justice and prosperity as confusing names and definitions.

To illustrate the question of what is real and what is not, Plato tells a story about a cave. In the middle of a cave, a number of prisoners sit against a small wall, chained there since childhood. They face one of the walls of the cave. Behind them there is a huge campfire that they cannot see. People walk between the campfire and the prisoners. All the prisoners can see is the shadows of these people on the cave's wall in front of them. And because of the echo within the cave, even the sounds the people make seem to come from the direction of the shadows. To the prisoners, these shadows are the real world.

Now let's assume, Plato continues, that one prisoner is released from his chains, gets up and walks around. At first, he will not recognize anything in this new reality, but after time he would adapt. He would understand more about the new world, and perhaps even understand how people walking alongside a campfire cast shadows on the wall. What would happen if he returned to the other prisoners and told them what he has learned? They would ignore him, ridicule him, and if not for their chains, probably kill him.

What Plato is trying to tell us is that a philosopher is like a prisoner freed from the cave, trying to understand reality. On a deeper level, Plato explains that the words we have for things refer to concepts in our mind; in other words, the shadows. We perceive reality through these concepts. Plato's Cave is an old story, but still told in many variations. For instance, Plato's Cave provides the philosophical basis for the film *The Matrix*, in which Morpheus explains to Neo: "How do you define real? If you're talking about what you can feel, what you can smell, what you can taste and see, then real is simply electrical signals interpreted by your brain."

Plato's Cave showed that what was reality to the prisoners was nothing but a shadow, covering the "true reality." For centuries, philosophers have tried to break free of their chains and find the truth. The Enlightenment philosophers believed the world was a large "machine", and it was man's purpose to uncover the laws of nature through reason and understand how the world turns. Immanuel Kant spoke of the Categorical Imperative in his search of universal principles to decide what's right and wrong. Throughout the Middle Ages, truth was a religious principle. Plato believed that everything we saw was just a reflection of an underlying concept, which Kant later called the *thing as such* (Ding an sich). Every tree is an example of the concept of treeness, every person an example of humanity, every chair an example of chairness.

We are Postmodernists

But the postmodernists try to break away from the idea of truth. In their view, there can only be perception. Everything we perceive comes to us through our senses. What we see, what we feel, what we hear, and so forth. Perceptions can be communicated and shared, but this only means that reality is a social construct and can change anytime. Because perceptions are shared through language, truth and reality are culturally dependent. Think of the legend that Eskimos have nine different words for snow, or that doctors, accountants, lawyers and IT specialists have rich jargons to describe their truths and realities in much more detailed terms than those in other professions. Philosophers that shaped postmodernism include Søren Kierkegaard, Friedrich Nietzsche, Ludwig Wittgenstein and Martin Heidegger. Although postmodernism has its critics as well, it is the dominant way of thinking today.

If we look through the postmodern lens, what more would Plato's cave reveal? Let's expand Plato's thought experiment. To my knowledge, Plato never said the prisoners were not able or not allowed to talk. Let them talk, and have them describe what they see. The prisoners sitting on the ends of the row may describe the shadows close to them as very long, while the prisoners in the middle would characterize them as short. The cave is warm to those sitting close to the fire, but cold to those sitting farther away from it. Each would tell a different story. And, just for the sake of argument, let's bring in time travel and introduce a video camera into ancient Greece. We'll allow all prisoners to record their view of reality and share those recordings. Whose recording is true? They are all true.[1] If they are smart enough, they will detect a pattern if they each describe their reality from left to right. In fact, let's take the experiment one step further, and allow the prisoners to turn around. They can see the fire and all the people moving through the cave, but are still chained to the wall. They would *still* each describe a slightly different view on reality.

In short, postmodernists wouldn't describe truth in terms of the shadow on the wall, and their underlying reality, they would describe it in *relative* terms; i.e., relative toward other perceivers regardless of whether they are looking at the shadows or the real people. In other words, truth is not in the objects we examine, not in the *things as such*, but in the eye of the beholder.

An Information Management Perspective

Although we live in the postmodern world, IT professionals (and many other business professionals as well) are firmly entrenched in classic times. In the tradition of Plato and Kant, there must be a universal underlying truth to things, and all we have to do is apply reason to uncover it. Sure, it may change over time, but hopefully only to move even closer to the "true truth."

It is in the field of information management that this

---

1 They are all true, although none of them real. A recording of a shadow on the wall is even one level more removed from reality than the shadow itself.

classic attitude is most visible. Professionals concerned with defining key performance indicators, putting together organizational taxonomies and building data warehouses have been looking for a single version of the truth since the advent of the information management discipline. It seems that most organizations have fundamental alignment issues in defining the terminology they use. In fact, I have formulated a "law" that describes the gravity of the problem: The more a term is connected to the core of the business, the more numerous are its definitions. There might be ten or more definitions of what constitutes revenue in a sales organization, what a flight means to an airline or how to define a customer for a mobile telephone provider.

Few have been successful in reaching one version of the truth. Business managers have fiercely resisted. Machiavelli might have pointed toward political motives of business managers since a single version of the truth would limit their flexibility to choose the version of the truth that fits their story best. However, IT professionals say business managers should see that the benefits of satisfying their own goals are less important than the satisfaction of contributing to the success of the overall organization. In fact, ignoring less important needs for the benefit of higher pleasures is a hallmark of human civilization[2]. So much for civilization if we can't even achieve this in the workplace.

Are IT specialists fighting windmills like Don Quixote? As I've discussed, the philosophers disagree whether there is a single objective truth or not.[3] Postmodernists go only as far as to suppose joint observations, but others come to the aid of the classical IT professional. The Ameri-

2 Like skipping dinner to be in time for the Opera. Or a man offering his wife his coat, so she can be warm instead of him.
3 As long as the philosophers haven't figured out whether there is a single truth or not, obviously there isn't one (or in all fairness, at least not one that we are aware of). But once we established there isn't a single truth, all of a sudden, there is one: the truth that there is none.

can philosophical school of pragmatism states that we can call a statement true when it does all the jobs required of it. It fits all the known facts; matches with other well-tested theories, experiences and laws; withstands criticism; suggests useful insights and provides accurate predictions. If this is all the case, what stops us from calling it "true"?

But let's stick to postmodernism for a while. To explain the failure of reaching a single version of the truth, postmodernists would point to the IT professionals themselves – they are simply misguided.

Solving the One Version of the Truth

By taking a post-modern approach to the single version of the truth problem that has been bugging information management professionals for such a long time, it simply disappears.

The reason why all these versions of the truth, often under the same name, exist in isolation is the vertically aligned setup of the management structure. Each business domain only reports up to strategic objectives, and most of the reporting is "self reporting," the domain reporting based on its own data.

However, using a process-oriented approach, horizontally aligned and next to each other, multiple versions of the truth actually make sense. The various departments or business units each have a different relative position in the value chain and, therefore, a different view on the current revenue or the number of customers. This doesn't mean that every single definition is valid and should be preserved – in fact, many definitions may be redundant. The real question is: How does an organization decide which definitions are valid and which are not? Valid definitions, placed in the right order, constitute "one context of the truth."[4]

---

4 The analysis on how to solve the single version of the truth problem is based on Chapter 6 of Performance Leadership (Buytendijk, F., McGraw-Hill, 2008).

Take, for instance, the revenue analysis I did in a software firm. A quick examination revealed the existence of definitions such as gross revenue, net revenue, net own revenue, recognized revenue, management revenue, total commission revenue, invoiced revenue, statutory revenue, taxable revenue and actual cash inflow. There were management reports for most of these definitions, but there was no management report in which these types of revenue were grouped into context. Yet, creating a comparative relative analysis of these types of revenue reveals analytical value. Analyzing the difference between gross and net revenue provides insight into the discount practices within the organization. This is still fairly standard.

But consider net own revenue, which excludes the revenue for licensed third-party components. If the percentage net own revenue decreases to a certain point, perhaps it is time to acquire the licensing company (or an alternative technology). Every salesperson should also be aware of the difference between net revenue and recognized revenue. Recognized revenue is the amount that may be booked into the current revenue based on bookkeeping regulations. Particularly interesting for salespeople is the total commission revenue, on which the salesperson's compensation plan is based. Ideally this adds up to management revenue, but there may be double compensations because of sales overlay structures. There also may be a difference between the software sales. For example, perhaps an additional discount was needed because of a missed implementation deadline.

Cash flow is important as well, as revenue can only be spent again if there is actual money in the bank. Salespeople should be aware of the paying behaviors of their customers. Lastly, salespeople should also see statutory and taxable revenue to understand the impact of their sales results on stakeholder value. By organizing the different definitions of the term revenue in a flow, we can see the existing definitions that make sense and lead to alignment as well as those that add to confusion. The former definitions should be kept and the latter eliminated. This revenue report, with its different definitions of revenue, has created the long-awaited single version of the truth... or rather, one context of the truth. There are no synonyms possible anymore because all terms appear in the same report, and the combination of these represents a single flow of revenue. Perhaps even more important, this style of reporting has a positive influence on the behavior of the account manager. Instead of revenue, the account manager is enticed to think in terms of contribution.

"What is a train?" is a more complicated question than you would think at first. Different stakeholders have different views. For a passenger it is the means for the journey to their destination. From a regulator perspective, a timetabled train is a line that runs multiple times per day, based on budget and policies on public transportation. The planning department would also add maintenance movements and empty trains scheduled to travel to a new departure point. Traffic control would look at actual – including unplanned – train movements. The infrastructure department might actually count slots, a time window in which a train is supposed to travel, and this might include other operators' trains as well. Through a horizontal alignment approach, organizing all definitions in a single report, the definitions become more transparent and comparable. There is value in analyzing the differences. It is important to minimize the difference between the demand plan and the operations. The difference is in planning efficiencies and the number of incidents and accidents. The closer the number, the more optimized the plan is. Then the difference between operations and the staffing plan needs to be minimized, allocating scarce human resources as efficiently as possible.

In the previous two examples, the one context of the truth was a value chain. In the case of a ratio, the context can also be a matrix. For instance, the average revenue per user (ARPU) is an important performance indicator in telecoms. One telecom operator I worked with distinguished between average invoice per user (AIPU), business ARPU, reported ARPU and analytical ARPU. Business ARPU is based on the AIPU, but includes interconnection revenues between operators (not visible on a customer invoice). Roaming users generate revenue too, which contributes to the reported ARPU and pollutes the ratio, as roaming users are customers from other telecoms. Not all revenue makes it to the reported ARPU – some revenue from foreign countries comes in after the reporting data. However, it should be still be allocated to the current period. This is called the analytical ARPU.

Defining an active customer is complicated. When do you start being a customer – when you sign the contract or connect to the network for the first time? When do you stop being active – when you only receive calls or text messages? When do you stop being a customer – after termination of the contract or when the warranty of the phone expires? What about prepaid users? If we create a single context of the truth, a different type of report emerges in the form of a matrix. From top to bottom, it would include various types of income such as fees, additional services, discounts, interconnection fees, corrections, and so forth. From left to right we would list active users, then total customers and roaming users. This matrix provides a new analytical insight – the *quality* of the revenue. The higher the percentage of revenue (fees and additional services from active customers), the higher the controlled revenue of the telecom provider. The higher the roaming revenue from other providers and the higher the other incoming revenues, the more you depend on others and the higher your uncontrolled revenue. This matrix serves as a risk management model as well.

How would you define "money transfer transactions" in a retail bank? Every retail bank has a vast array of reports around the number of these transactions and their monetary values, broken down by business unit, product and most probably geography. But how many reports would there be that combine those definitions to closely align the various steps in the money transfer process? The report would start with how many customer contacts throughout the various channels kick off a money transfer (without necessarily completing it). The next step would be to distinguish money transfers between customers' accounts, between bank customers (both not requiring a clearing house) and between banks. Some transactions will be rejected for various reasons – the account is over-drawn, the receiving bank does not accept the transaction because of missing or incorrect information, the account is blocked or the account no longer exists. When counting transactions per week or per month, there might be differences as well. Transfers have a transaction date, a clearing date and an interest date. Counting transactions using any of these dates will lead to different results per period. Even after the transfer is completed, the actual process continues until all information is correctly reflected in the bank's general ledger. If we analyze the multiple stages in money transfers and detect patterns, we can derive predictive value from the one context of the truth. Sudden changes in customer contact moments can predict workload later in the process and consequences for the cash position reflected in the general ledger.

All these examples provided a demonstration of how taking a relative and horizontal view solves the single version of the truth problem. We can start separating the wheat from the chaff. In other words, creating a relative view on the truth helps dramatically reduce the number of reports and definitions. Many different definitions have been created for historical reasons, political reasons or because people were not aware of any other relevant definitions. With the one context of the truth, every business department will see where it adds value in the chain and each can concentrate on the definitions that make the most sense.

Moreover, horizontally structured management information can provide greatly improved insight into an organization. In the software company example, understanding how to define revenue – which allows account managers to understand the financial consequences of their operational sales decisions – can lead to changed behaviors that are more fully aligned with strategic objectives. In the railway company example, gaining deeper insight into operations is possible through a horizontal value chain and a methodology that provides an understanding of what drives operational efficiency. In the mobile telephony company example, breaking out average revenue per user helps us evaluate the quality of revenue and gain deeper insight into what average revenue per user actually means. In the retail banking example, transaction volumes can be predicted by understanding existing patterns and using forecasting algorithms.

Could it be that Simple?

How can a problem that a field full of intelligent people has struggled with for twenty years be so simple to solve? This cannot be true. There must be a catch to it. Let's explore this a bit further. The problem itself is forced by one of the most dominant paradigms in business, the hierarchy. Information management as a discipline is shaped very hierarchically, and creating alignment is mostly a vertical exercise – it is hard to escape the central paradigm of a discipline. With all best practices being hierarchical of nature, we are not naturally challenged to question a hierarchic approach. The solution I am describing here is neither unique nor new.

Creating horizontal alignment – aligning the value chain – is the core competence of professionals in business process management (BPM). They do not have the single version of the truth problem at all. Transactions in processes typically are a single version of the truth. In fact, BPM suffers from the opposite problem – how to deal with *multi-reality*. Sometimes, truth changes during a case, affecting the outcome of the process. Updating pension plans based on marital status or changing employers can take notoriously long. Applying for health care benefits, based on taxable income, can be horribly complex as taxable income often has multiple stages of determination. The problem BPM professionals face is how to complete a process that is fundamentally based on a single version of the truth when the underlying truth changes. Information managers and process managers should talk more with each other. But specialists often offer great depth within their discipline, without knowing much of other disciplines. Conversely, generalists have an overview of multiple disciplines, but may not have enough insight to tackle specific problems. Solving fundamental problems such as the single version of the truth or handling multi-reality requires some deeper thinking by both specialists and generalists.

Life is What Happens When You're Busy Making Plans
Throughout this piece I have been playing with the terms truth and reality. The more you think about it, the harder it seems to distinguish the two. It is not easy coming up with examples of something that is reality, but not true, or vice versa, without really thinking it through. Traditional philosophers have an easy job here; they could say that reality is a manifestation of deeper-lying truths. But post-modernists have a hard time. Still, there is an important difference between reality and truth for them as well. To demonstrate this, I will rely on *truths of fact* and *truths of reason*. This distinction was made by German mathematician and philosopher Gottfried Wilhelm Leibniz (1646-1716). A truth of fact is based on observation. For example, if there are three apples on the table, and others observe the same, we call it a truth of fact. For me, truths of fact are synonymous to reality. Reality is based on observation too. But there is more to truth than reality. Truths of reason follow the path of logic, but this doesn't always have to be reality. For instance, any probabilistic statement, such as predicting rain for tomorrow, doesn't have to become reality. And sometimes, following logic just leads to absurdity. "I fit in my coat, my coat fits in my

bag, therefore I fit in my bag" is logically completely true, but not very realistic. Trying to create a single version of the truth doesn't bring you closer to what's real. In fact, the post-modernists reason it will only lead you further away from reality.

So... every time you are studying a graph in a management reporting system, or you look at a process description, you are simply watching shadows on the wall. To paraphrase John Lennon: Reality is what happens when you are busy defining truth.

It's an Analytical World

"In God we trust; all others bring data."
— W. Edwards Deming

Bringing an analytical view to business is one of the most significant business trends in the last decade. Almost every job profile requires analytical skills, business intelligence has been at the top of the CIO agenda for many years, and fact-based decision-making is the business model for a complete industry of consultants and analysts. In fact, I have been in analytics for all my career as well.

Competing on Analytics: The New Science of Winning, by Davenport and Harris, has become a very influential book. The authors argue that outsmarting the competition is the biggest distinctive capability for organizations in the years to come. They provide a roadmap to becoming an analytical competitor, describe an analytical process, provide insights in how to manage analytical people, and spend time on how to define the right technology foundation.

This idea is not new. Frederick Taylor is well known for introducing scientific management in the early twentieth century, particularly in production environments. Most of us will immediately remember Charlie Chaplin's "Modern Times" movie, which took productivity improvements to the absurd. In World War II, *operations research* came to be, including techniques such as simulation, decision trees, linear programming (maximizing results while working with limited resources), and dynamic programming (e.g., to find the shortest route for deliveries). These techniques are the basis of today's analytical toolkit.

Originating in the medical world, *evidence-based management* is now becoming popular. This movement also suggests the use scientific methods for making decisions, but evidence-based management also includes the attention to ethical considerations and a focus on behavioral economics. Behavioral economics breaks with the widespread idea that people make rational decisions as proposed by decision theory, but instead are influenced by a wide variety of circumstances. By better understanding these circumstances, behaviors and decisions can be influenced.

What could be against this approach? CEOs are responsible for their employees and their families; we wouldn't want them to make far-reaching decisions based on their gut instincts. Although intuition, experience and other soft factors may play a role, at the minimum they should be tested and validated before an actual decision is implemented. So how can we make the best of analytics?

Analytical Philosophy

The old philosophers would have loved this direction that business decision making is taking. According to the dictionary, analysis is nothing more than "the separating of any material or abstract entity into its constituent elements" – taking something apart in order to understand what it is, what it does, what elements it has, and how these elements relate. Analytics is the science or process of doing all this. This is a core competence for philosophers. They take fundamental questions or concepts and break them down into smaller questions until there is a certain understanding or logic revealed. IT people would call this process "functional decomposition."

The love for analysis that philosophers display is only logical. Many of them were mathematicians as well. Aristotle (384 BC – 322 BC) formulated the laws of logic. Gottfried Leibniz (1646-1716) and Sir Isaac Newton (1643-1727) invented calculus independently of each other. Rene Descartes (1596-1650) was the father of Cartesian geometry. Over the years, philosophy has become increasingly analytical in nature. In fact, led by Bertrand Russell (1872-1970) and Ludwig Wittgenstein (1889-1951), a large part of twentieth-century philosophy is known as *analytical philosophy*. This branch of philosophy creates formal logic including a notation (language), based on the analysis of language, to create clarity of argument. You could say this formal logic is very much like what SQL is to databases. In fact, in a narrow sense, this school of thought rejects the idea of thinking big thoughts and examining the fundamental purpose of life. Analytical philosophy proponents state that philosophy is nothing else but trying to create logical clarification of thoughts. IT people would call this "requirements analysis" and "building the query."

Let's explore what we can learn from the philosophers here.

Do We Think, Or Do We Know?

You would think that people promoting fact-based decision making and a more scientific approach to management would base those recommendations on, well... facts. In a recent article in the *Journal of the Academy of Management*, researchers found in a large meta-study (analyzing the available studies) that the evidence for evidence-based management was poor and anecdotal at best. Or consider another example. Good academic papers always have a "limitations" paragraph in which the shortcomings of a research design are described, or under which conditions the conclusions are valid and under which conditions they are not. Business literature rarely has such disclaimers. On the contrary, the sky is the limit.

Perhaps the best recent case of unlimited skies comes from *Wired*, an influential American technology magazine. In 2008, editor-in-chief Chris Anderson wrote an article called "The End of Theory: The Data Deluge Makes the Scientific Method Obsolete." Although it wasn't clear if he was being provocative or was actually serious, his central thesis was that in the near future we will no longer have to create models for analyzing phenomena. With computers already powerful enough, we will simply feed it all the data there is without the need for any context or hypothesis. The computer will do the statistical analysis and provide an in-depth description of reality instead of a theory. As Anderson noted in the article, "With enough data, the numbers speak for themselves." In science, we are taught that correlation doesn't equal causality. It is necessary to understand the underlying mechanisms –

just a correlation could be a coincidence. However, if we have all the existent data, there is no room for coincidence. Every single case, every instance simply has been covered. We could ask the computer to analyze all the data and see what it shows, what descriptive algorithms it comes up with. Anderson uses examples from physics, biology, and other fields to point out that more advanced technology has already created more precise descriptions of reality for the last centuries. Why not foresee the last step?

The early Enlightenment philosophers would have been on Anderson's side. In the Age of Enlightenment there was an unshakeable belief in technological advancement. Benedict de Spinoza (1632-1677) asked if there would still be a need for God if everything that happens in the universe can be explained in scientific terms. Newton didn't see that contradiction–he posited that God created the universe and now it is up to us to figure out how it works. The metaphor of the universe in those days was that of a machine, albeit an incredibly complicated one. But even the most complex problems can be solved if you unravel them bit by bit.

"Do we think, or do we know?" is a famous quote from Gary Loveman, the CEO of Harrah's Entertainment. He uses this question to test if a proposal is truly fact-based or "just" a good idea. But it raises an interesting question. What do we really know? What is really true? It seems like every philosopher has explored an angle to these important questions, but for the purposes of the subject of this article, I have chosen the most relevant angles. Gottfried Leibniz (1646-1716) identified two types of truth: truths of reasoning and truths of fact[1]. Truths of reasoning simply follow logic, such as if A is true, so must B. If all cows are mammals, then one particular cow must be a mammal too. If there are four apples on the table and you divide them equally among two people, each gets two apples.

Alternatively, based on reasoning we can be sure that

---

1 Also see "The Myth of the One Version of the Truth"

certain statements are not true (or at least not so far), such as "The deaf person turned around when he heard footsteps", or "I recently had an interesting chat with a dead man." Truths of reasoning are hard to dispute or deny. This is the analytical world. You create a model, based on one or more hypotheses and/or available data, and start to build in rules for how the model works. The logic can be described and transferred to other people as well. A model can be called correct (or not), and the outcomes can be predicted just by examining the rules, even before actually running it. In other words, truths of reasoning can exist before the event – *a priori*.

Then there are truths of fact. These are based on direct observation. I could claim there are four apples on the table, but in fact there might be only three. I could claim I lost four kilos in the last three weeks because of a new diet. This can only be observed if I stood on the scale three weeks ago, measured my weight, and stood on the scale just now. But who is to say the loss of weight was caused by the diet alone? There might have been other reasons as well, such as stress, sports or anything else. And did I lose those kilos in a somewhat linear sense, or did I gain a kilo and lose five over that period of time? Truths of fact can only be measured after the event – *a posteriori*.

You could object to the use of the terms truths of reasoning and truths of fact. What is a fact anyway? We can observe only through our senses, namely sight, hearing, smell, taste and touch. As postmodernists most of us agree that as a result there are no real facts, just interpretations. And if you measure through some kind of recording device, such as scales, sensors, computers, video or audio equipment, the observation is limited by the capabilities of the device. It would only measure what it is designed to measure, based on a concept of reality that exists in our minds. It might measure precisely, but does it also measure completely? The British philosopher John Locke (1632-1704), although a product of the Enlightenment, also agreed there is always room for error. Even if a phenomenon is observed by multiple people, it can still be wrong, as people's senses are limited.

Locke's observations also invalidate Anderson's reasoning in the "End of Theory" article, notably based on Anderson's own arguments. Locke observed that even carefully constructed knowledge over the centuries turned out to be untrue, or imprecise. As insight grows and technology progresses, we simply discover more layers of complexity. As Anderson describes, quantum mechanics corrected Newtonian models and there are many discoveries to be made in the field of genetics. Perhaps a simple example is our insight that the earth does not contain only four elements: air, fire, earth and water. Who can truthfully claim that if computers capture all the data, it is really *all* the data? We just don't know. And even if we did, data still doesn't equal reality. The best we can claim is that results are probable.

So truths of fact are not that factual. At least we still have truths of reason, right? But in the end, a model is always an abstract of reality. And even if we could construct the perfect model, as Anderson claims, the outcome of running such a model can only be as precise as the data in it – the truths of fact – and these cannot be validated.

In short, truths of reason can be true, but can be based on false assumptions. Truths of fact can never be true, only probable. Reality has its own unpredictable ways. As the joke goes among economists, "Reality is the exception in the model." So the reliability of data collection and data analysis is problematic. After careful analysis and weighing all the facts, the only answer we can give to Gary Loveman's question is, indeed, "I think." What is there to know, really? No wonder philosophers are not the most popular guys on the executive floor – before you know it, you can't rely on anything anymore.

Perhaps there cannot be such a thing as truth of fact, but at least it's the closest thing to truth we have. Surprisingly, help comes from another era – the Middle Ages. William of Ockham (c. 1288 - c. 1348) was an English Franciscan friar that today is best known for a principle called Ockham's razor (although this term was not his). Ockham's razor is the idea that "entities must not be multiplied beyond necessity" or "plurality should not be posited without necessity." In other words, if there are several hypotheses on how to explain a certain phenomena, you should favor the hypothesis that contains the fewest assumptions and has the fewest elements. Go for succinctness. The use of the term "razor" means that in formulating a correct hypothesis, you need to shave away all unnecessary complexities. Although "the simplest explanation is often the best" may be a bit too simplistic, this is how Ockham's razor is usually paraphrased.

What follows from this is that the more you are removed from actual measurement (a truth of fact – although the postmodernists would disagree) and the more you stack up assumptions (truths of reasoning), the more likely you will be wrong. This all seems pretty theoretical, but there are many practical implications. Let's call, for practical purposes, a direct observation or measurement zero-steps-off reality. The moment we do something with that information, such as combine it with other information to create a ratio, aggregation or any other kind of calculation, it is one step off reality, and the probability that the result is not precise increases. A calculation based on a calculation then would be two steps off. The more steps off you are, the more you need to rely on truths of reason that might be inherently correct, but don't match with reality.

Seen this way, profit is a measure of success far removed from atomic measurement of costs, revenues and other components that ultimately lead to establishing profit. There are many assumptions involved in determining the actual profit, even within highly standardized accounting rules. As a result, profit is simply too unreliable to assess the health of a company. Cash flow is close to direct and unambiguous measurement, and as a result much more reliable. Or, consider an equally prominent performance indicator that is even less defined: customer satisfaction.

It doesn't tell you that much, as it is often a composite of many factors. Things that can be directly measured and that *drive* customer satisfaction, such as on-time deliveries, the number of products returned, complaints, and repeat orders or referrals, tell you much more.

The problems associated with truths of reason can have widespread societal consequences.

Remember the 2010 eruption of the Eyjafjallajökull volcano in Iceland that led to shutting down airports all over Europe? Airplanes could be in danger when flying through a cloud of volcanic ash. The problem was that there were no actual measurements of ash particles; the decision to close the airports was based on meteorological models that predicted the distribution of the ashes. In the meantime, this was costing airlines $200 million per day. Truths of reasoning were used where truths of fact would have been appropriate.

The same can be said of the 2008 credit crunch. Banks would buy packages of collateralized debt with a certain risk profile, would use amazingly complex financial models to chop them up and repackage them, and would sell them off again. At no point in that process did the transaction hit the real business model of a bank. It was pure speculation. Once reality changed (subprime mortgages not being paid off anymore), the model broke down and a chain reaction occurred. Again, truths of reasoning were used where truths of fact were needed.

Predicting the Future

"It's hard to make predictions, especially about the future." This quote has been attributed to many, ranging from author Mark Twain to baseball legend Yogi Berra to Danish physicist Niels Bohr. Not a very good start when turning to predictive analytics. If we can't predict the future, predictive analytics is a misnomer. The easiest way to explain this is by using an example we all know. When we rehearse a conversation in our heads ("... if they say this, I will say that"), that's predictive. When after the conversation we tell ourselves, "Darn, I should've said that," that's analytics. You see, the term is problematic.

However, predictive analytics is the hottest of analytical topics in the market today. (Admittedly, predictive analytics has a nice ring to it; something we'd all like to have.) Actually, there is not much new under the hood. All the underlying statistics, data mining techniques, operations research and game theory principles have existed for many years. Predictive analytics is just another label. In this type of analytics, we can distinguish predictive models, descriptive models and decision models. Predictive models look for certain relationships and patterns that usually lead to a certain behavior, point to fraud, predict system failures, assess credit worthiness, and so forth. By determining the explanatory variables, you can predict outcomes in the dependent variables. Descriptive models aim at creating segmentations, most often used to classify customers based on sociodemographic characteristic, lifecycle, profitability, product preferences and so forth. While predictive models focus on a specific event or behavior, descriptive models identify as many different relationships as possible. Lastly, there are decision models that use optimization techniques to predict results of decisions. This is sometimes also referred to as "what-if" analysis.

Although predictive analytics sounds like a very scientific field, its Newtonian approach is problematic. The English-Irish philosopher and member of Parliament Edmund Burke (1729-1797) remarked that our society is so big and so complicated that a single mind cannot possibly understand how it works in its full complexity – let alone make predictions about it. Furthermore, it changes continuously and organically, not like a machine at all.

Let's reconsider Chris Anderson's article about the end of theory in this light. If we collect all the data in the world, and construct the perfect model, indeed we can run every correlation we can think of or – more importantly – the system can think of. These correlations then describe the relationships (but should not be confused with causality) in the data. Per definition, data comes from the past, and we can only measure what is already there. This means the correlations are retrospective in nature as well. In the end, there is only one thing we can say about the future: there is a high probability that it will different from today. This way you can argue that running analytics actually invalidates the predictive value of the data. The only thing you can predict using predictive analytics is in situations when there is no change. That's not much of a prediction.

Even rock-solid science shows many examples of sudden, radically changing patterns. Take, for instance, fractals, a set of mathematics that relies on recursive equations (a formula that uses itself again...and again, and again). Starting out fairly predictably, soon their complexity becomes endless. Two very similar fractal expressions can lead to extremely different results in just a few iterations. Fractals are used to describe shapes in nature, such as clouds, mountains and rivers. They are also used for data compression and even for art.

Nassim Nicholas Taleb, a professor in risk engineering, former Wall Street trader and author of The Black Swan, uses this example to describe reality in society as well. Taleb argues that change doesn't happen gradually, which is the assumption that most of us work from, but rather in "jumps," controlled by "the tyranny of the singular, the accidental, the unseen and the unpredicted." Gradual change is our paradigm, yet actual change is "almost always outlandish." Taleb refers to these events as "black swans." This was a common expression in 16th century London to describe an impossible thing, as obviously swans are white. However, in 1697, Willem de Vlamingh led an expedition on the Swan River in Australia and actually found black swans. The term then started to mean something deemed impossible, but found to exist. Taleb uses the term to describe hard-to-predict, rare and high-impact events beyond what we could normally expect. And these black swans appear all the time. Think of the H1N1 or SARS epidemic in global health, the collapse of

Enron in business, the credit crunch in 2008, or positive things such as the invention of text messaging. And who knows, next year we may learn about a cure for cancer, a way to store massive amounts of energy in a small pill, or discover there is alien life. Our world will never be the same again.[2]

Taleb argues we do not live in "Mediocristan," the world we understand. We live in "Extremistan," where sudden developments in many different areas can have immensely disruptive consequences. Given the diversity of black swans and the fact they happen all the time, it doesn't make a lot of sense to trust our models of reality, even the perfect ones. Disruption is always around the corner. We keep falling for it because of a few fallacies. First of all, we learn by induction, which means we draw general conclusions from observations and experience. As we cannot know what we don't know, we are not ready for "exceptions to the rule." Second, we believe that history repeats itself, so we only look for change we know. Third, we seek meaning in events and invent explanations after the fact, which is much more comforting than staring at sheer randomness. Taleb specifically warns experts – who claim they understand their area of expertise and use massive amounts of statistics – to offer insights to support their conclusions. Experts in particular tend to underestimate the uncertainty of events.

So if we can't even trust the experts, who (or what) can we trust?

Messy Analytics

In the analytical world, truths of reason have become truths of fact. You don't get a credit card if the major source of income on your bank account does not equal in-

---

2 Then again, there are always long-term megatrends. IT adoption increases despite many hypes and disruptive technologies, illiteracy decreases, oil becomes more scarce. You can bet on those trends strategically, but you will still have to respond to black swans tactically.

come code '03' (I am just making up an example here). You don't get good car insurance if you have the wrong ZIP code. Your flight gets canceled if the weather model predicts ashes from a volcano eruption. "Computer says no." The analytics of the models have become so complex that we cannot do anything but believe the outcome of them. Consider the cause of the credit crunch – financial analytics chopping up and repackaging subprime mortgage packages. The analytics themselves (the truths of reason) have become the product itself (the truth of fact). All this occurs while, per definition, a model of reality and reality itself are not in sync. This is a recipe for disaster. Even so, we manage the nice and clean logic of the model, instead of coping with the messy reality.

I am not suggesting we need to get rid of analytics. People suffer from bounded rationality – our brain capacity is insufficient to oversee complex problems and come to rational and optimized conclusions. Computers are a great help in better decision-making. However, as reality is messy, I suggest we adopt what I call messy analytics. This means various things.

First, when you do statistical analysis, resist the temptation to remove the outliers. Improbable scores or data are usually filtered out of the dataset because it is noise "messing up" the model. However, the outliers might actually represent the most interesting bits. They could be the early warning signal for a black swan coming or could represent new business opportunities that others – following best practices –neatly filter out. If the model is your lens, you won't see any change coming. You won't get any weird new ideas. What you see is what you've always seen. All the model does is confirm your hypothesis. Outliers deserve extra attention.

Secondly, I strongly suggest actually intentionally introducing noise to the model and the analysis. This is based on a principle called *perturbation*. If you throw a "wrench in the machine," the people in the process need to figure out how to deal with that disturbance. In the case of an analysis, the analysts would have to figure out what that really means. Or, in the case of a learning algorithm, how the system would explain the noise. As the future cannot be predicted, the only thing you can do is be ready for it.

Deliberately introducing disturbances helps people train for the event when real change is occurring (e.g., a fire drill). A real-life application of this can be found at airports. The X-ray machines are programmed to show forbidden objects in luggage, and it is the task of the security person to notice those objects. Missing too many of them means the officer is not sharp enough! The same thing should be done in analytics as well.

Furthermore, there should be more qualitative research. One effective methodology is scenario analysis. The principle is very simple. Create between two and four scenarios that list the major assumptions that the business model is based on (such as increasing prices, decreasing costs, or limited or abundant availability of a certain resource), and reason what happens if this assumption all of a sudden doesn't hold true anymore. Scenarios are narratives that describe how your organization will be doing in such an imagined world. Instead of narratives, you could also create computer games, in which you need to act in such a possible reality. Again, the aim is not to be right about the future, but to be ready for it. The narrative is not supposed to be precise and complete, but it should be imaginative and provide a call to action.

Other types of qualitative research include ethnographic research or even participative research. One insurance company I know of has videotaped customers going through customer interactions with the company, not only recording action and time, but also body language and other types of soft data. In fact, "Undercover Boss" is a TV show in the United Kingdom and in the United States, in which a CEO of a company goes undercover and works in the front lines for a few weeks, learning about the real work and real problems of the employees. This is quite a different approach from drilling down in a productivity report.

Scientists will be quick to point out the *Hawthorne Effect*, which explains that measurement itself already impacts the behavior of the subject that is studied. The term comes from the Hawthorne Works, an American factory that conducted a series of worker productivity experiments in the 1920s. One of the tests focused on the impact of the illumination in the factory on the workers' productivity. They found that better lighting improved productivity, which was expected. However, they also found that dimming the light or leaving the lights alone also improved productivity. Indeed, it was the people walking around measuring productivity itself that impacted the productivity. This is a curse for science because you try to study a subject as objectively as possible and don't want to alter behavior. You can't control all variables, and there are no truths of reasoning in this style of analysis. You mess with reality, but then again, hopefully reality messes with you too and you learn something.

Perhaps the most straightforward advice I can give is to simply talk to people if you want to figure something out. Don't send surveys, as they only measure the things you thought of and rule out the possibility of serendipity. Talk to people. Ask customers and partners what they like about you and what not, and ask suppliers if they find it easy to do business with you. Ask your staff how they are doing, and how they think the company is doing.

Messy? Certainly, that's the good bit. It's as close to truths of fact as you can come.

A Just Business or Just a Business

Computer says "no."

Running gag about customer service
UK comedy series "Little Britain"

In life, work and society, we depend on IT. We need IT to organize our lives, to do our work, to use basic utilities such as electricity, for most of our amusement and so forth. With the popularity of hand-held devices, more and more activities in our daily lives become IT dependent. But how many times do we ask ourselves if the way IT permeates our life is *just*? For instance, how do we treat the mental health of our employees in our business processes? How do we really add value to the lives of our customers? Do we have obligations to our suppliers? To what extent is an organization a money-making instrument for shareholders? In trying to optimize our business, are there any limits in analyzing data?

Questions of right and wrong are the domain of moral philosophy. *Morals* (or *ethics* – the terms are often used interchangeably) form a code of conduct to refer to in judging what is right and what is wrong. Ethics revolve around three central concepts: *self, good,* and *other.* You display ethical behavior when you do not merely consider what is good for yourself but also take into account what is good for others. This does not mean that you should be completely altruistic and always do good to others without considering your own needs. That is not sustainable. Moral dilemmas arise when the division between what is ethically right and wrong gets blurred.

Obviously people can display ethical or unethical behavior, but we also think of organizations as ethical or not. Organizations are living organisms as well. They are born, grow up (some never do) and die. They create offspring, in the form of business units. They make decisions and display unique behaviors, both functional and dysfunctional. Given our definition of ethics, every organism that displays deliberate behavior – as organizations do –

should be judged on its ethics. Examining organizational ethics is a popular subject – in leadership and in governance, no doubt largely driven by the trend of *corporate social responsibility* (CSR).

Some doubts, or even cynicism, about CSR are appropriate because – in all honesty – CSR and ethics are merely paid lip service in many organizations. This is not because top management has a hidden agenda or malicious intent. In fact, I believe most top managers truly mean what they say about being socially responsible. It just doesn't happen because the operations are simply not organized for it. Henry Mintzberg, one of the world's leading authorities on strategy and business, wrote in 1983: "The economic goals plugged in at the top filter down through a rationally designed hierarchy of ends and means … [The] workers are impelled to put aside their personal goals and to do as they are told in return for remuneration. The system is overlaid with a hierarchy of authority supported by an extensive network of formal controls … Now, what happens when the concept of social responsibility is introduced into all this? … Not much. The system is too tight."

Looking at the core control model of organizations, there are two layers: the operational layer and the management layer. The business processes are housed in the operational layer, and most organizations have the goal to optimize the cost, speed and quality of these business processes. Cost, quality and speed are the three pillars of what is called *operational excellence.* Typical business processes are order-to-cash, procure-to-pay or hire-to-retire. In the management layer, there are decision-making processes, for instance around planning (plan-to-act), reporting (record-to-report) and strategy (design-to-decide). These processes are largely driven through an analytical approach and aim to optimize an organization's ability to change. The keywords of what is called *management excellence* are smart, agile and aligned. Being smart means seeing and understanding change within the organization and in the market a bit better and faster than others, agile means being able to make the necessary changes to capitalize on new insights, and aligned means being able to copy those new ways of working throughout the value chain to prevent suboptimal solutions that benefit only one department or function.

Let's explore the consequences of Mintzberg's observations and have a closer look at the ethical side of business processes and analytics.

Ethical Business Processes

It is not unusual to consider the ethics of certain business goals and business practices. These areas are quite directly connected to the question of what is "the right thing to do." In fact, most large organizations have a relatively strict code of conduct on how employees are to behave. However, I have never heard of ethical considerations when designing a process.

On the philosophical level, for me, a process is a promise. A process promises that if you use it, the outcome will be timely, predictable, and correct. What complicates matters in most organizations is that processes are often obligatory. You have to use them not only for reasons of control and compliance, but also for efficiency.

Sometimes a process itself cannot live up to the promise for a variety of reasons. Perhaps the necessary management approvals are too slow, people operating the process regularly miss customer deadlines, or the output is unpredictable and the systems supporting the process behave like a black box (computer says "no"). People who need to operate these processes may start to display certain dysfunctional behaviors, for instance frustration and anger. In fact, there are many documented cases of people hitting or destroying their computers or even harming people. Another effect that a bad process can have is lethargy – people stop caring about the outcome and lose their sense of accountability and responsibility. In almost all cases, people find ways to trick or even circumvent the complete process. For instance, they might fill in information that allows the process to continue, instead of inputting all of the information that is needed to complete a high quality transaction.

In these cases, the process becomes dysfunctional because it is badly designed (not with the right goal in mind), because it was designed for different purposes (such as too much emphasis on compliance instead of operations), or simply because the processes are executed badly. The question is if we can call these processes unethical. Are they morally approvable? One definition of being unethical is not conforming to approved standards of social or professional behavior. The keyword here, of course, is "approved." There is a subjective sense to it, but it is clear that the behaviors that the process triggers are not according to certain standards of social and professional behavior. Still, the effect might be unintentional.

Let's consider another example, coming from a discussion I had while teaching a class of MBA students. I argued that one of the most important performance indicators for a claims department of an insurance company would be the processing speed. I reasoned that a claim rejected, fast and well motivated, would lead to less customer satisfaction than a claim paid out after months. One of the students, working in insurance, shared that this was not how they were looking at it. They would be very happy to delay payment to unprofitable customers, hoping that customer satisfaction would indeed drop and the customer would leave. In my opinion, that is a clear violation of the business model of an insurance company. An insurance company is a collective of insured people that each pay a little bit to compensate the few who need compensation. This means that the profitability comes from the collective, not from the individual. If you extrapolate the reasoning of the student, the mere moment there is a claim, profitability for that customer is hurt already, and claims should be avoided for all customers at all times. Obviously complex and large claims require more checks, correspondence and other activities that would delay payment and therewith negatively affect the processing speed. Perhaps it makes sense to segment claims into different categories of complexity and decide which average processing speed would be appropriate for each category. However, I think most people would agree that deliberately slowing down claim payments with the intention of driving unprofitable customers away is not a standard of professional behavior and is unethical.

Business processes can also be unethical because of the behavior they trigger in others. Take, for instance, Nike, now a leader in corporate social responsibility. A *Harvard Business Review* article described the journey the company traveled to become so widely recognized for its CSR practices. The company recognized that its responsibility included the practices of its suppliers as well, and Nike initiated audit teams to check on factories allowing child labor, among other things. The company found it hard to prevent child labor in supplier facilities, not because of unwillingness of the supplier, but because of another Nike process. The Nike procurement department was fully focused on cost optimization, and incentives depended on optimized costs. Although there is always a choice, Nike's procurement practices made it hard to stop the practice of child labor. It was only after procurement and auditing aligned its processes and incentives that Nike sent a clear and effective signal to its supplier base.

Now, consider the role of technology. The goal of technology is to amplify human abilities – at least that is one way of looking at it.[1] A bow and arrow extends our reach, a telephone our hearing, the Internet improves our sight and communication skills, a hammer amplifies our strength, and so forth. If we use technologies to build systems that do the opposite, that reduce human abilities to do a good job, then we use technology in an unethical manner. Think, for instance, of the movie "Modern Times," in which all that Charlie Chaplin had to do,

---

1 Also see "Technology, What Have You Done for Me Lately?"

standing behind a production belt, was to tighten a screw of each product passing by. Although I think most of us believe those modern times are way behind us, in fact most administrative processes very much still look like this. Most business processes and business applications are optimized towards operational excellence through extreme standardization.[2] People are put behind a system with a thick manual and extensive training on how to operate the system, and then are asked to process a stack of transactions. Every day.

During a doctor's appointment, doctors often spend more time entering data into their computers than they spend talking with the patients. Customer service representatives spend all their time behind their customer relationship management system and call scripts, instead of actually talking with the customers to understand their needs and requirements. Back office employees fill in endless screens with completely predefined processes, typically based on the exception to the rule, such as fraud detection and so forth.

There is a complex relationship between desirable and undesirable behavior triggered by business processes and systems. Let's consider the example of enforcing labor laws. Some countries have laws to protect employees from work shifts that are too long, and it is not allowed to work longer than, for example, 10 hours a day. To make sure employees follow this rule, it may make sense that the HR system in which worked hours are logged daily creates a setting that prevents people from entering more than 10 hours of work per day. However, if people work in different countries, or the job simply calls for longer hours, they may end up working longer. If the system prohibits entering the real number of hours worked, people will find tricks and workarounds to fill in hours (booking hours on the weekend) or start building their own spreadsheets

2 Still very much like Scientific Management, or Taylorism, popular in the 1930s.

to track reality. In this case, an ethically correct rule may trigger unethical behavior.

Or consider the system a police force uses to enter data of people being apprehended into custody. I know of one case where the rules didn't allow recording the ethnicity of arrested people. Still, the police felt this was relevant information and used another field no one saw the need for – shoe size – to code ethnic background. Many entries displayed shoe size 99, 98, 97 and so forth, the numbers corresponding to a code for ethnicity. There are no ethical issues with the process or the system, but people who really want to circumvent rules will always find a way.

In general, dumbing people down and reducing their work capabilities to simply operating the system in which every action is preprogrammed is the opposite of what technology is supposed to do. Technology is supposed to amplify human capability, at least by taking tedious work away, so people can concentrate on higher value tasks.

In manufacturing, for many years we have been aware that processes shouldn't harm the health of workers, and in office environments we make sure people have comfortable chairs and can take a break once in a while. But what about the mental health of workers driving administrative processes? Business processes should have positive effects on users, driving the right behaviors and, quite directly, productivity.

For instance, a good business process could create what psychologists call a "flow," a state of mind in which a person is fully focused on and immersed in a certain activity, where time seems to fly and the work even seems effortless. An ethical business process also provides immediate feedback so that employees can see if what they are doing is indeed the right thing. In well-functioning operational environments, people are also included in decision making and planning. This creates buy-in and people feel appreciated.

Business process users should also have a certain degree of autonomy on how to plan and execute their work. After all, they are the ones who have direct interactions with customers and are the first ones to see patterns of change in the market through the large number of transactions they handle. Particularly when there is a wide variety in the type of transactions, a system should allow its users to master their discipline (which is something entirely different than mastering the system). For instance, the system may provide suggestions, but it should be possible to skip unnecessary steps, or – the opposite – flag and escalate specific cases. Lastly, there needs to be a purpose, an understanding of why the business process is important. This is particularly difficult – and important – when processes have been consolidated in huge shared service centers, performing large batches of transactions disconnected from a real customer or real result. Providing flow, feedback, inclusion, autonomy, mastery and purpose creates a situation in which people care.

Enabling people to care about results obviously is not a business goal in itself, nor is it fluffy and soft. In fact, motivated and caring people directly contribute to hard and tangible business results. Autonomy and flow affect productivity. Mastery and purpose are key contributors to organizational agility. Feedback and inclusion are the cornerstones of quality improvement.

One example of how business processes reinforce corporate ethics comes from an insurance company Interpolis. The insurer has "Crystal Clear" (translation) as its motto. It means doing business with Interpolis should be really simple. The company truly lives this motto in everything it does. I get an annual overview of all my insurances on a single sheet of paper. Reading the conditions is significantly easier than I am used to, as the company carefully looks at the language it uses. A few years ago I reported a stolen laptop. I called the insurance company to request claim forms and inquire about the process. The friendly lady in the call center asked me for the brand of the laptop and how old it was. She immediately told me the amount I would get for it and indicated the money would transfer to me within a day or two. She asked me to keep the police report, in case my claim was included in a random sampling of claims to be checked. I was amazed; it was really simple to work with the insurance company. They built their processes to cater to the bulk of transactions, not the fraudulent exceptions.

Ethics of Analytics

The world of operations is dominated by process, and data is dominant in the world of management. Data is stored and is waiting to be analyzed to see if, for instance, operational targets are ambitious enough, or whether a certain operation needs optimization, or – on a strategic level – to see if the organization still has the right operations. Like operations, analytics are very much driven by technology. This becomes particularly apparent when technological constraints are lifted because of technological breakthroughs. If capacity or speed is limited, most questions revolve around on *how* to achieve a certain insight.

However, if all of a sudden capacity or speed are unlimited, the question left is *why* to acquire that insight. Whenever technology lifts constraints, moral aspects arise: It may be possible, but is it *right*?

Let's consider some examples. Imagine you are an analyst at an insurance company, and you read somewhere that sitting behind the computer too long is bad for your health. It can lead to neck and back problems. Your interest is sparked. Additionally, you've also been part of a very successful project initiating a customer community on the company's website. Through this website, for which you need to register, you can discuss and rate medical specialists. is the website also has a large database of health and diet best practices. In a moment of creativity, you decide to write a small program to track which customers spend the most time on the website, and you correlate that information with the claims data in the data warehouse. Indeed, you find a correlation! These people clearly are a higher risk, which should be reflected in their insurance premiums.

Is this an ethical analysis? Is it morally acceptable to mine for this correlation in the data? It's data, it can be analyzed, and it leads to more knowledge. What can be wrong with that? Still, I would guess that there is a good chance you'd intuitively consider this analysis wrong in some way. Why is that?

Maybe it helps to use another example using the same insurance company. Instead of writing a little program tracking how much time customers have spent on the community website, you post a survey there, as part of a preventive health program. You ask people questions about time spent behind the computer and any possible neck and back problems they may have. As a thank you, after submitting the survey, customers receive a computer program that warns them every 45 minutes that they should do some stretching exercises. They can view a short video of an attractive man or a woman performing those exercises and can easily join in.

Would this be ethical to do? Again, it's data that can be analyzed, and it leads to more knowledge. What can be wrong with that? My guess is that most people intuitively feel there are no big issues with this initiative. How is this different from the previous example?

One difference that is immediately obvious is that in the first example there was no *consent*, but there is consent in the second example. In the first example, customers trustingly visit the website, use it for all kinds of community purposes, but don't expect this data to be used for other purposes. In the second example, there is consent; people willingly complete a questionnaire. Thus, if there is no consent to use data for a specific analytical purpose, there may be ethical issues.

Let's now consider a third example. Mining the data warehouse of the insurance company, you find that a sizable percentage of customers who upgrade their dental insurance, claim dental expenses that originally weren't covered in the two months after upgrading. You recommend that the marketing department change the terms and conditions, and let coverage of newly covered claims start after four or six months. Are there any ethical issues with this? Again, I have found that not many people would have issues with this recommendation. In fact, it is a fairly common precaution in dental insurance.

Also in this case there is no consent, but in this case we don't see an issue. What is different? In this third example, there is malintent from the side of the customer. The customer knows that dental work is coming and quickly upgrades the insurance so that it is covered. The only thing the insurer is doing is protecting its fair interests. So next to consent, *intent* plays an important role.

In the third example, it was the intent of the customer that made a difference, but the intent of the insurance company is relevant too. What made the first example (mining website data) problematic was not only the lack of consent, but also the intent. People are invited to join the community website, and they are invited to stay as long as possible to peruse the wealth of content on the site. After having done that, they may face higher premiums because of having developed a higher risk profile. It's a trap, and clearly not ethical. In the second case, not only is there consent (filling in the survey), but the intent is different as well. The intent is to provide preventive help for avoiding the development of neck and back problems.

Hang on, you may say. Isn't the whole point of business to make your business as sticky as possible, and then maximize the business value with each customer? What do morals have to do with that? Neoclassicists would argue that the market solves issues like this automatically, as customers simply go elsewhere. Although that is all true, again it is intent that makes the difference. If the intent is to create a sticky business because of superior customer value, then there is no ethical issue. If the intent is to simply extract as much money as possible for as long a period of time as possible (for instance, overpromise and underdeliver), this might be morally questionable.

Being confronted with questions like this, what would

make you decide to either perform a certain analysis or not or, after the fact, what to do with it? Would you check if it breaks the code of conduct that you signed (or industry regulations, or even laws)? Another way of reasoning would be to imagine what would happen if customers would find out that you have business practices they feel are unethical. In fact, there is a general rule that says: When reviewing an email you'd like to send, always consider how it would look on the front page of the *Wall Street Journal* (WSJ).

There are two schools of thought in philosophy that both feel they have something to say about it. First there are the *universalists*. They feel that things are either fundamentally right or wrong. If lying is wrong, then it is always wrong, even when it is for "good reasons." They would only accept intrinsic motivation (something being good or bad), regardless of rules and the front page of the WSJ. Regarding analytics, they would say you should only ask a question if you are truly prepared to know the answer. Then there are the *consequentialists*. They believe it cannot be said up front if something is good or bad because that is determined by the outcome of a certain action. In their view, the analysis itself is not ethical or unethical, but rather what you decide to do with it. If any analysis leads to better business for both customers and the organization, it is fine; if it leads to disadvantaging customers, maybe not (unless they are trying to take advantage of you!).

But at least, the universalists will appreciate the possibility of asking yourself these questions before constructing a certain analysis. After all, if you start asking these questions after having performed the analysis, all that is left is the consequentialist approach: What are going to do with this new knowledge?

Interestingly enough, this is exactly what breakthroughs in IT are accomplishing. In-memory databases provide unprecedented performance, speeding up a typical analysis from hours to minutes or even seconds. Storage has become so cost-effective that it is no longer necessary to decide what data to store and what to discard. With all the analytic power we have, it becomes easier to correlate everything with everything, on the spot. But if analysis is performed at the speed of thought and is associative of nature, there is nothing that at least makes you stop and wonder if this is the right thing to do.

In fact, the situation is even more complicated. Analytical tools have made a big jump forward. Normally the only thing that could be automated would be the known questions, the known processes, and the known analytical questions. But with data mining tools crawling through the data warehouse and other data stores, analytical tools also start to answer unknown questions. This can lead to problematic results.

Imagine you have a data mining tool running all kinds of analyses, and the tool reports to you on a daily basis what interesting things it has found. For instance, it finds a correlation between customer profitability and something like "Immigration Center" as an address (in various European countries, immigrants from certain countries stay in a center first before their application is evaluated).[3] How would you react? Would you feel comfortable discouraging those customers from doing business with you? Would you feel comfortable if this report somehow leaks to the press? Undoubtedly most people would find this an extremely sensitive analysis.

The interesting thing is that no one asked for these kinds of analyses, but as they are presented, you cannot undo that new knowledge. Can there even be a universalist approach? Or has technology ruled out a complete school of thought? The question "is this the right or wrong thing to do" is completely irrelevant because it is done already, and no one decided on it.

---

3 This actually is a real example from a bank that indeed started to discourage these customers. It made the newspapers, created an uproar, and the bank quickly reversed the initiative.

The only question that remains is what you are going to do with that knowledge – the *intent*. You can throw the report away, but in that case the system also doesn't learn anything. It might suggest the same analysis next time, and suggest it to others as well. Something I have never seen in a business system, but what could be interesting, would be a "This is not OK" button that would put certain correlations on a black list. The basis of such a list, of course, can be created up front, the universalist would argue, but it is realistic to assume that there will always be combinations that you haven't thought of before. Still, it is somewhat unsatisfying, as this is still an action after the fact. Even the consequentialist would not be happy with this solution, although he would feel the only thing that counts is action after the fact, because telling the computer not to come up with this correlation anymore also prevents the company from doing something good with the analytical result. Like the CEO of a large bank once said: "There is no such thing as an unprofitable customer, there are only unprofitable business models." A better business model could be created, which means that as sensitive as a certain analysis is, it would still be useful to know.

This is the moment where the universalist, recovered from the technology progress shock, chimes in again. A general rule, ethically defendable, is to state that you can't and shouldn't stop progress. There are always good and bad ways of applying knowledge, and the only way you can battle bad applications of knowledge is by knowing even more about (unintended) consequences of action and how to counter bad applications of knowledge.[4]

Now What?

Currently, over one-third of the 100 largest economic entities in the world are corporations, not countries. Whether you embrace the principles of CSR or not, corpo-

---

4 For more discussion, see "Technology: Can't Live With It, Can't Live Without It"

rations have a large impact on society. As societies have created "social contracts," so do organizations in the form of CSR reports. One of the world's leading strategy professors Michael Porter explains how shareholder value and CSR do not have to conlict, CSR is a way to create competitive differentiation and competitive advantage.

Unfortunately CSR today is often equated with being "green." Although there is nothing against green initiatives, they miss the point. CSR ultimately is about being ethical in everything you do. Personal behaviors do not suffice; organizational strategies do not suffice. As Mintzberg pointed out, it's the bit in the middle: management and process.

Management and process... after ethics being discussed on the level of leadership and governance, this is the where the next ethics discussions should take place.

Soft and fluffy? I don't think so. I think this is the path to true sustainable business performance. As the CEO of Indian service provider HCL argues in "Employees First, Customers Second," well-treated and well-behaved employees take superior care of customers, and the shareholders will have no reason to complain.

Social Analytics: Your Organization (and Society) as a Collective Intelligence

"Resistance is futile."
Star Trek: Borg

If you ask anyone to describe the organization in which they work, chances are he or she will draw an organization chart for you. It will list business units, departments, people in charge, and it will look like a well-balanced hierarchy. This is how people are managed in the organization. Others, perhaps the more enlightened ones, will draw a value chain, structuring the various activities that the organization performs to add value. It will show how procurement and warehousing support production, and how production aligns with logistics and sales and marketing, all supported by HR, Finance and IT. This is how work is being managed throughout the organization.

Complex Adaptive Systems

Both views are correct, but both views describe only a very limited aspect of what an organization really is. Boiled down to the essence, organizations are complex adaptive systems. They are dynamic networks of all kinds of interactions and relationships, and these relationships and interactions are continuously shifting based on tiny (or bigger) internal and external changes. As a whole, a complex adaptive system continuously adapts and learns. At best what you have is a fragile equilibrium. In most cases, the organization will operate far from these optimal conditions because of the energy required to manage the continuous change. This also explains why every organization is unique, even when it has the same strategy as another organization. External changes in the market trigger different changes within the system of the organization. Organizations evolve.

See if you recognize the following behaviors or patterns in your organization:

- Sometimes it feels like decisions just emerge. No one can remember having said "yes" or "no" to a proposal, yet as a group we seem to go a certain direction.

- The moment the competition makes a move, you huddle to see how to respond. You know from your contacts working for the competition that they huddle when they hear you huddle in an attempt to figure out what you huddle about.
- You may have heard of "high-performing organizations," but your organization seems far away from it. Keeping up with change, let alone driving it, is quite an effort already.
- The best strategies and ideas you can remember came from groups of people with very diverse professional backgrounds. One of those moments of magic happened when sales, marketing, IT and legal evenly contributed.
- It's not what you know about the business, but who you know in the business.
- When you boil it down to the essence, it seems there are only a few factors that you use in analyzing what is going on in the organization, and you are usually right.
- Planning is a mysterious activity. After a few iterations, every relationship with reality seems to be based purely on coincidence.
- Our organization seems to be in a constant state of reorganization.
- Creativity seems to come from the smaller business units, far away from headquarters.
- The more I dig, there is always one additional layer of complexity.

The more you recognize these situations, the more you confirm your organization is a complex adaptive system, as they translate into the properties that are associated with it: emergence, co-evolution, sub-optimal, requisite variety, connectivity, simple rules, iteration, self-organizing, edge of chaos, and nested systems.

The Organization as a Living Organism

Examples of complex adaptive systems include markets, organizations, ecosystems and most living organisms, such as human beings. To zoom in on one particular parallel: organizations can be compared with living organisms. Like people, organizations are born, grow up, and die. Some barely grow up; they die young and irresponsible. Other organizations mature and grow old and wise. Like people need oxygen to breathe, organizations need cash. Over time, organizations expand and sometimes contract, like people who gain weight and diet when necessary. Organizations, like people, create children in the form of new activities and business units that sometimes spin off into other activities and units.

There is an academic field focused on this approach, organizational behavior (OB). OB is the study of how people behave within organizations and, one level up, how organizations behave within a complete social system. OB relies on a system approach for the study and application of knowledge about how people, individuals, and groups act in organizations. This is the process of understanding how things influence one another within a whole.

In fact, groups (and as a consequence organizations) can display their own behavior, without being able to directly track this back to the behavior of a single person or element. Consider this famous experiment that has been described in many different ways over the years. Eight monkeys are put in a cage, with a bunch of bananas hanging at the top of a stairway. After the first monkey climbs the stairs, the other monkeys are sprayed with water. It doesn't take long before any monkey climbing the stairs gets beaten up by the others. Then, one monkey gets exchanged for another, who gets beaten up the moment he attempts to climb the stairs, without knowing why. Another monkey gets exchanged, and the same thing happens. After all monkeys are exchanged, no monkey dares to climb the stairs to get to the bananas, without a specific reason for avoiding the stairs. The group displays behavior as a whole.

Consider another example. The US Navy has multiple aircraft carriers, and the largest of these are called super carriers. Between five and six thousand people work on such a ship, and every 18 months the majority of staff is replaced. Despite the heavy job rotation, every one of these super carriers is known for having a distinct culture, independent of the behavior of each of its individual crew members.

Organizations, being complex adaptive systems, have unique behaviors and develop a collective intelligence over the years, again independent of each of its individual members. The collective intelligence of an organization can be seen as the body of knowledge about the business and its market that is stored within the organization and somehow gets passed on to new organization members.

Collective Consciousness

French sociologist Emile Durkheim (1858-1917) and Swiss psychiatrist and psychologist Carl Jung (1875-1961) took the idea of collective intelligence a few steps further and came up with the idea of collective consciousness. This is the collective sentiments, morals, conceptions and perceptions that the average citizens within a certain community share. People are bound to the norms and values of their environments, in which – as social beings – are doomed to exist. Personal behavior cannot be explained without the context of the environment from which they come. Jung came from a different angle. He discovered that people around the world share rituals, without being connected to each other. According to Jung, these rituals come from primal experiences that are passed on.

Inferring from here, it is no coincidence that religions have some version of what Christians call the Ten Commandments. Morals are roughly the same all over the world. You shall not kill, you shall not steal, and so forth. You can argue that morals are meant to protect the collective consciousness, as it cannot live without its inhabitants – human beings.

Here is where we need to be careful. When googling "collective consciousness," you are never more than two mouse clicks away from an esoteric "new age" approach, or references to "The Secret" that explains how everything in the cosmos is connected. Interesting perhaps, but not usable for our purposes here.

Still, facing the danger to float away on a pink cloud, it is important to examine the idea of a collective consciousness a little. It is a logical and evolutionary thought. The first many centuries of mankind revolved around a collectivist approach. Survival, poverty, religion. The industrial age changed it all, and we live in individualistic times now, focused on wealth, self-actualization and science.

Individualism leads to suboptimal results. It has been successful so far because prosperity took away so many constraints that the suboptimal nature of everyone creating the maximum result for their own good alone did not limit growth. But in nature, individualism is not looking for synergistic results where the total result is more than the sum of the parts. The logical path of synthesis between the collective and the individual view is to find a way to connect individuals (despite the current countertrend of social and economic polarization).

Moreover, the concept of collective consciousness solves an important issue of philosophy: the kiss of death of postmodernism. In order to explain what I mean here, I need to take a few (big) steps back.

Man was the First Modeler

When mankind became conscious, it meant humans could distinguish themselves from the world around them. But there was a price to pay. It also means that we, human beings, are not fully part of the world anymore. All we can do is perceive what is going on around us and try to make sense of it. You could say that man was the first modeler.

Since the beginning of philosophy, people have tried to build a mental model of the world based on truth. We would identify objects, label them with names, and come up with all kinds of attributes to describe those objects. For instance, a cow has four legs, it eats grass and it has multiple stomachs. It can have a black and white pattern, but can also be brown. It has a certain DNA structure, and all these things together create an object called cow. This type of thinking lasted until into the Age of Enlightenment, and science is still full with it. The universe acts according to a certain set of rules, and all we have to do is discover them. Still, there is plenty to discover, even in hard sciences. For instance, to explain the increasing pace of expansion of the universe, the vast majority of required matter to fuel that expansion is simply unaccounted for. There are forces at work we don't even know yet.

But in the twentieth century there was a turnaround to something we now call postmodernism. We realize that all we can know comes through our senses. As our senses have limited capabilities, our model of the world is limited by nature as well. We cannot state that a cow has certain attributes. We can only say that we see something that so far we have called "cow" and that we perceive some common elements. All attributes have moved from what we thought to be an object and a part of reality to a categorization in our mind. The things we see in what we call a cow (so far). Nothing more. Truth has disappeared in this way of thinking and has been replaced by a "sufficiently shared view." The shifting of attributes to label and name things is not very uplifting. It means we are all alone in our perception of the world. Furthermore, I find it practically unacceptable: How can we function? Even a sufficiently shared view is not helpful because all we can do is perceive that. Postmodernism is a death trap. Once you have the thought that there is only perception, there seems to be no way out. And if you don't agree with me, that is just your opinion.

The idea of collective consciousness offers a way out. It combines the ideas of truth and perception. Perhaps indeed all attributes of an object or concept exist only in the mind; but if they are shared through a collective consciousness, there is a process of replication and inheritance that makes sure we all have a similar way of perceiving and categorizing. As we are complex adaptive systems, we may have different ways of qualifying things. Some see a cow as a steak-to-be, others see it as something to trade or to get milk from. Some like cows and others don't.

This process replication and inheritance doesn't have to be "magic," in which we are all "tapped into" a greater structure. British scientist Richard Dawkins came up with the idea of *memes*. A meme is an idea, behavior or style that spreads from person to person within a culture. Being an evolutionary biologist, Dawkins observes that this process is constantly evolving, like trends. Ideas, behaviors and styles change over time and keep spreading. However, the process is somewhat different than in the well-known children's game where the first child in a circle whisper's a sentence in the next child's ear. At the end of the circle, the sentence has changed completely. Because everyone is communicating ideas all the time with everybody else, the story "averages out," and a good level of common truth emerges.

In this sense, the collective consciousness is an even better idea than both classical truth and postmodern perception. Truth evolves over time, like a complex adaptive system itself. The collective consciousness connects people, but there is also room for alternative and differing opinions.

Back to Business

If organizations possess a body of knowledge that is transferred like memes and creates a collective consciousness to which members of the organizations belong and identify with, it would be great if we could somehow capture that with technology. Technology's aim is to augment human capabilities (at least that is one view on the essence of technology), and this would be a huge augmentation of capabilities.

Knowledge management (KM), popular in the 1980s and 1990s wasn't "it." Although no one ever said that KM should be a top-down process, this is how it turned out in many cases. The project team and the team running KM were responsible for uploading all documents, feeding the search instruments, creating a central taxonomy and so forth. And, like most information management initiatives, KM highly mimicked the corporate hierarchy. Not ideal for creating a maximum buy-in throughout the organization. As most people already have their informal networks to get the information they want, there really is no need to use the corporate system. Corporate intelligence doesn't equal collective intelligence.

The bottom-up approach was also often not very successful. Why would knowledgeable employees contribute to a knowledge management system and "give away" the asset that makes them unique and valuable? In fact, I heard of one example of a consulting firm that tried to promote its knowledge management system by publishing a top 10 of contributors and rewarding them for their contributions. With adverse effects. The list became known as the "losers' list" and the "bench-sitter list," consisting of people who obviously had time to do all this, in contrast to the important consultants who did the "real" work.

"Connecting individuals," one of the central ideas of the collective consciousness, is also the core of social media. It would certainly explain the popularity of social media worldwide. Twitter and Facebook have become an integral part of our lives and give us a sense of security from being connected with the people around us. Social media shows what is important to others, and it leaves it up to our imagination what to do with it. In essence, social media platforms are superconductors for memes.

But are social media platforms the right tools for creating "wisdom of the crowds," to use a more modern term for a collective intelligence? The data coming out of social media is unstructured, fragmented, usually highly ambiguous and lacking context. Social media may have most of the characteristics of a complex adaptive system; but social media, as they operate now, are also not "it."

Social media platforms are perhaps sufficient for private use for the time being, but they need more attention when using them in business. We need to find a way to fuse the structure of knowledge management with the dynamics of social media.

Simply adopting existing social media platforms and implementing them within your organization under the label of "Enterprise 2.0" is not enough. Any democratization of communications will lead to a quality-leveling effect, concurrent with massive expansion of communications. There most likely will be more knowledge sharing through forums where employees can discuss with each other, but that is still a few steps removed from a collective intelligence, let alone a collective consciousness.

First of all, there is still a need for focus and leadership. New strategies and ideas won't come "automagically" through the wisdom of the crowds. A new style of leadership needs to be accepted. Influence and power in a networked environment doesn't necessarily come from the ones at the top, but from the ones that are best networked and possess the best insights and credibility. Influence comes from different sources. But still it takes leadership to channel discussion to make sure all aspects are covered. Discussions through social media often lead to new and unexpected angles, but not necessarily to all relevant angles.

Leadership is also needed to keep focus in a discussion. A bottom-up and widely democratized discussion digresses easily. This is fine in blog comments, on Twitter, Facebook and other social media for private use, but not very helpful within an organization that wants to stimulate a collective intelligence and consciousness. A conscious entity is able to imagine a situation, a future, and plan a way towards that future. This is also the essence of strategy within an organization. An unmoderated discussion easily leads to what is called *strategic drift*. If strategy is seen purely as a process of emergence (which is one school of thought in strategy), taking an incremental approach typically causes the organization to easily drift away from its original direction. Or even worse, the organization gets nowhere because the discussion is all over the place and nothing gets implemented.

Bringing an action orientation to the discussion also requires leadership. Particularly in broad discussions, covering a wide variety of angles, there is a danger of *analysis paralysis*. This means no decisions are taken, as the phase of gathering and interpreting information is endless in nature. At one moment, the decision needs to be taken to stop discussing what to do, and either start discussing how to do it or hand out marching orders to get stuff done. (Even in today's world, it eventually boils down to this.)

But understanding how to use technology is not enough. The technology itself needs to evolve as well to add to the creation of a collective consciousness. The word "consciousness" is direct from the Latin word *conscius*, which means "having joint knowledge with another." In philosophy, if not debated, the term is used to describe experiencing perception and being aware. This means we should not only have the means of sharing information and knowledge with each other, as we do now using social media, but we should also get feedback on that process so we are aware of the process of knowledge sharing and its effects.

We can only imagine the analytical power that social media companies such as Facebook, Google and Twitter use to data mine and text mine the enormous amounts of data. On a very personal basis, they know what we talk about and with whom we talk about it. They know the brands we like and even capture significant amounts of our online behavior outside the use of the social media. On an aggregated level, this could help with overall sentiment analysis (how we feel about the economy, how accurately we predict the next winner of The Voice, or if we can predict social unrest in a particular neighborhood or country). This analysis could also provide insight into how common memes have become to see if they represent a common truth. The problem with these analyses is not that they are not available; the problem is that they are not aimed at the public (with the possible superficial exception of Twitter trending topics). They are aimed at the true customers of the social media companies, the advertisers. These analyses certainly add to a high level of intelligence, but their current value lies in their exclusivity, not in their collectiveness. It is not in the best interest of the current business model of the social media companies to change this and open up extensive analytics to the public, sharing the created consciousness.

In conclusion, business needs to get this right for its own sake, leveraging knowledge across the organization and creating a strong culture and body of knowledge less dependent on the specific people inside the organization. But moreover, business needs to get it right from a social responsibility point of view. Although the popularity of social media has been driven more by the consumer market than by business, the chance that business will drive the innovation in creating social media feedback is greater, simply because there is more alignment in the business model.

After having done that, the enormous wealth and power of social analytics should be used for the good of society, actively building the collective consciousness. I am sure there is a great business in doing that.

1

What is Your IT Philosophy?

> *"Questions about my thinking are not foolproof, but if I or someone else can raise issues about my thinking, if I can dig down for the reasons or arguments underlying my thinking, if I can look clearly at objections, if I can follow the good arguments where ever they lead, then my thinking may be improved and I may reduce the degree to which I fool myself."*
> *-Socrates*

What is your IT philosophy? An easy question to ask, but very hard to answer. If you ask a CIO for his or his philosophy on IT, chances are the response will be "to keep things simple" or "buy, not build." Although these are fundamental insights or principles, I am not sure if I would really call them an IT philosophy. The word philosophy is often used in the sense of an "approach." But philosophy is more. It is a discipline that looks for a comprehensive view on reality. Philosophy requires systematic reflection.

There is a philosophical branch called "philosophy of technology." This branch actually dates back to the days of Newton, when science started to have a greater effect our daily lives. The actual term philosophy of technology was used first by German philosopher Ernst Kapp (1808-1896). Martin Heidegger, Karl Jaspers and Karl Popper are other very influential philosophers in the field. However, the term "philosophy of technology" has only been adopted broadly since the 1980s. Most of the work has focused on either understanding the principles of engineering, viewing technology as a topic of its own, or on the impact of technology on society. Futurist and cyberpunk visions dominated the popularization of philosophy of technology. Unfortunately, the philosophy of IT – as a subset of technology – isn't as well developed.

I do see an important need for a specific philosophy of IT, with a special focus on governance and ethics. Business is often seen as an amoral practice (not immoral).[1] Its aim is to maximize shareholder value, and not utility, happiness, or any specific virtue. Corporations are legal structures more than societal entities. The interaction between business and society is based on an exchange of money and therefore is values-free. In this view, there is no need for a philosophy of IT (or business technology, to use another emerging term). IT is a part of business and serves the goals of business.

Increasingly this view is opposed. Stakeholders want more from business than money. Employees seek meaning and a place to develop their professionalism. Customers (and suppliers) identify with the brand. Even within the economic system based on shareholder value creation, morals play a role. Shareholders certainly don't want to see the businesses in which they invest to be immoral – granted this is probably mostly for reasons of reputation risk mitigation. In economic terms, immoral behavior increases transaction costs between businesses, leading to higher prices and lower margins. Trust is an important economic principle. I did some early work on something called the "true value index" (TVI)[2], in which I argued some profits can be damaging the business, such as profits coming from squeezing suppliers (they weaken the value chain) and profits based on market opacity (they open up space for competitors).

If business is moral and should be governed in a moral way, then IT – as a ubiquitous business practice – has moral aspects too. In discussing this, let's stay close to economic principles and examine what drives value.

Value has two sides. It needs to be provided and it needs to be received. If the supplier feels real value is provided, but it is not perceived that way by the customer, there is no value. There needs to be a shared understanding. This idea is the core of what is often called business/IT alignment. Many organizations are struggling with this. There seems to be continuous contention between these two "sides." Business managers typically feel that IT is lagging behind and cannot

---

1 No wonder business has a trust issue. We can only put trust in people or other organisms that display moral behavior.
2 Journal of Management Excellence, February 2009

deliver. IT feels that managers do not know what they want and should get their act together before blaming IT.

Between two parties, one offering value and one receiving value, there can be (at least) three types of value drivers. The party offering value can be in the lead in driving value, and the receiving party recognizes the value. The receiving party can be in the lead, and the offering party strives to fulfill the requirements. And the relationship itself can also be the basis. It's not one or the other in the lead, but the combination of the two that creates the value.

Business and IT alignment problems, inhibiting creating and receiving value, start when there is no common ground on the type of relationship both parties have. If IT feels it is driving the value and invests heavily in innovation while the business treats IT as a utility, no matter how innovative new IT solutions are, the benefits will not be reaped. If the business is looking for value based on relationship, while IT is just interested in cost reduction and infrastructure, business will get frustrated. If both parties don't understand there are fundamentally different views on how to create and receive value, both will get confused.

Once there is a common view on how to create value, the actual value can be created. Again, there are different ways of doing that. Some see IT as a utility that should simply be there at a low cost. Others see IT as an enabler of better business, and yet others see IT as one of the drivers of entirely new ideas that can become the basis of competitive differentiation. These three views can be loosely coupled to one of the most dominant models in strategy, called the three value disciplines. These are operational excellence, product innovation and customer intimacy.[3] Although these value disciplines are meant for businesses as a whole to choose from, they can also be applied to IT

---

3 Treacy and Wiersema's value disciplines build on the work of Michael Porter, who indentified two core strategies: cost leadership and differentiation. Over the years, others have identified more value disciplines as well, such as brand mastery and customer lock-in. However, the model with the three value disciplines still has global recognition.

value. Operational excellence has a lot in common with IT as a utility. Product innovation and IT as a driver are related, and IT as a driver requires a certain (internal) customer intimacy to work.

IT as a Utility

Many business and IT professionals see the ultimate future for IT as simply being a utility. In this view, information should be available like water. The infrastructure is complex, requires serious investment and needs maintenance, but is essentially not our concern. This is the basic idea of the cloud. We upload our systems and their data, and we simply switch them on. The moment we need more storage or calculation power, it is automatically there. The invoice follows later based on your actual use. Like water, we all make use of the same infrastructure, but use it for our own purposes – to drink, to do the dishes, to brush our teeth, flush the toilet, water the plants, you name it – at a moment we choose ourselves. The cloud, like water and other utilities, should be multi-tenant in nature. Proponents of this philosophy see IT mainly as an infrastructure and not as a set of applications. The infrastructure has standard components to be used, reused and combined to match most people's wishes. IT as a utility should provide business with optimal choice, flexibility and freedom.

If this is your IT philosophy, you can call yourself a utilitarianist. Utilitarian philosophy argues that in the way we govern our world, we should strive for the greatest amount of "good" for the greatest amount of people. The two most influential contributors to this school of thought have been Jeremy Bentham (1748-1832) and John Stuart Mill (1806-1873). In some way, you can think of utilitarianism as a precursor to democratic thinking and a reaction to feudal societies, aimed at creating the greatest amount of good for just a small group of people. "Good," in terms of the utilitarianists, means fighting evil and pain as much as we can, and striving for the most pleasurable of circumstances for all.

Utilitarianism basically works as a decision-making

model. Whenever you have multiple options on the table and you need to decide between them, you pick the one that has the most positive effects on most involved stakeholders.

These are great guidelines for an operational excellence IT strategy. It requires your services to be available, easy to use, reliable and cost-effective. This means that as many people as possible can use them, afford to use them and use them all the time. Not only should an operational excellence IT strategy lead to as much use of IT services for everyone, but it should also minimize the pain for the greatest amount of people. So, for starters, IT systems will focus on automating menial tasks, for instance by optimizing straight-through-processing rates.

What possibly could be wrong with that? Well, learning from history and society, it could very well become the most totalitarian IT strategy thinkable. Who gets to decide what is the greatest amount of good for the greatest amount of people? All the people in the company, all the customers, and all the other stakeholders? The chances that a decent IT strategy will emerge from that are pretty slim. It will be a small group of people deciding, and the systems they introduce will be a standardized best fit for the masses, but will leave the smaller user groups and the niche applications untouched or forced into the big picture. This may fit some organizations that only offer commodity products and services, but a "race to the bottom" is hard to sustain as margins keep decreasing.

IT as a utility, taking our cloud example to heart, would only work if we infuse a good bit of liberalism. This means that people should be free to do whatever they want, as long as they don't inflict any harm upon others. Governments should not interfere with liberty, even not to protect someone against him/her self. That is everyone's own responsibility. There is a fine balance. Sure, smoking is your own choice (unless you believe the tobacco industry deliberately makes you addictive while you are young and still susceptible to such influence), but indirect smoking harms other. Driving a motorbike without a helmet is dangerous, but it is your own responsibility. However, accidents can also involve others. Yet, within this balance, independence is an absolute right.

Translated to IT strategy, it means IT should focus on infrastructure only and keep that as open as possible. In this philosophy, getting the right applications, serving the needs of many, as well as the many different needs, should be left to the business. IT is there to support them and take care of the system integration.

When business is in the lead, this strategy usually results in a very small internal IT function, with most of IT being outsourced. In looking for the right solutions, business will also be looking for cost to be as low as possible so that it can switch providers when needed to lower costs. When IT is in the lead in the relationship, IT makes itself very vulnerable. IT will have a hard time competing against outsourced alternatives; and in further attempts to lower cost and effort, business may take the lead.

This matches operational excellence. It is there, it is reliable, it is cost-effective. It takes problems out of the way. Either business can be in the lead (looking for low switching cost, outsourcing) or IT can be in the lead, usually when there is great distance between business and IT. This is a vulnerable position. The moment business takes the lead, internal IT will be outsourced.

It looks like an IT operational excellence strategy downplays the importance of IT and treats it as a commodity. When either IT or business are in the lead, this may certainly be the case. However, if the relationship itself is leading in creating the value, IT can be a strategic asset. The goal of the IT strategy could be aimed at creating competitive differentiation through high agility. After all, strategic investments in IT infrastructure mean that the business can keep all options open. It can integrate new technologies the moment they are available. By having things like master data management in order, by having a well-developed data warehouse and an omnipresent business rules repository, changes are made only once while immediately affecting all related aspects of the business.

IT as an Enabler

We often say that IT is not a goal. It facilitates the business and is a means to enable the business. This sounds very insightful and realistic. It shows that as IT people we understand the business, but what does it really mean? IT is a means, but so are capital, labor, materials and facilities (like buildings and machines) – in other words, all factors of production. Putting it in stronger words, you could reason that IT actually is part of overall facilities, and therefore what we saying is that facilities are facilitatory. Are we saying nothing?

That is not entirely true. When IT is seen as an enabler, it means it doesn't exist for its own sake. The value of IT is a derivative and is only exposed through better business. This makes a lot of sense, certainly from an Eastern philosophic point of view. Where Western thinking has always concerned itself more on objects and phenomena and their characteristics, Eastern philosophy has focused more on understanding relationships between objects or phenomena.

Think of it like this: a shape, like a box, a triangle or a circle, can only be identified by its borders, where it touches the rest of the world. Without borders, it has no shape, no identity, no existence. Without borders, it would be all, and therewith nothing. This is at least a view where existentialist philosophers like Karl Jaspers (1883-1969) and Jean-Paul Sartre (1905-1980) would feel comfortable with.

Something can only exist because of its boundaries. Existence is a specific being in contrast to the complete being of the world. These boundaries are dynamic, and not eternal. Existence is a continuous conflict between multiple forces that are in permanent opposition to each other, yet define each other precisely as a result of this opposition. The tension, or relationships, between those forces manifest themselves through interaction (mixing borders), confrontation (clashing forces) and communication (expressing their nature through each other).

You can only describe a phenomenon – like value – and express its nature in relationship to something else. Existentialism has its roots in nihilism, so there is no "value in itself." The world is amoral in that sense. "Bless you" is a term you wish someone else, or it is passively used on yourself, be blessed. Identities arise purely in relation to other identities. The master cannot exist independently of the slave. The supplier cannot exist without the customer. IT cannot exist without the business.

Friedrich Wilhelm Nietzsche (1844-1900) felt there is no fixed state of being, but a constant state of becoming. Out of nothing, a person needs to shape himself to what he or she is. This is not as bad as it sounds; it calls for positive action. People should engage the world. Through action a man can determine his values. Existentialist thinking requires no God or any other higher being.[4] You need to respond to yourself and to others.

In business, today we would call this holistic thinking, or systems thinking: the process of understanding how things influence one another within a whole. Unfortunately, we can never understand the whole world. Our horizon is too small. We can at best understand the interactions with the objects, the parts of the world that touch us.

It is hard to deny that in the end "everything is related to everything" and we simply are bounded in our rationality, but this is also a pitfall. It shouldn't mean that we give up on building the business case and try to find causal effects to express IT value. Another pitfall is that we get stuck in expressing all we do through the unique relationships that we have. The forces of interaction, confrontation and communication may be unique, but the elements may be completely generic. There is no need to

---

4 This doesn't mean you should not believe in a higher being. It is just not required to follow the line of reasoning.

come up with your own system and standards for book-keeping, for instance. Most CRM systems will look pretty much the same and simply require some configuration to be able to handle some specific interaction. "Not invented here" syndrome should be avoided at all cost in an IT-as-an-enabler philosophy.

When the business is in the lead in this strategy, it may very well lead to quick problem solving. Every action is seen in relation to a specific business problem and treated as such. IT, as a business subordinate, may develop a "your wish is our command" attitude. This may even be seen as very positive. IT people see themselves as business experts and identify more with the corporate brand than with their IT profession. Also, IT is extremely business-case driven. The result can be disastrous, an accidental architecture at best, with extreme fragmentation in the technology landscape.

With IT in the lead, the opposite result may be the outcome. IT tries to provide value and convince the business of its value. However, the benchmark or the requirement doesn't come from the business; it must come out of another relationship. This relationship may be with a dominant software vendor ("We're an SAP shop") or – more conceptually – may be based on all best practices in the world. The resulting IT strategy then may be one of standardization to cater to those external requirements.

However, if the relationship is in the lead, IT as an enabler can lead to extremely visible results. In fact, most new business models we have seen to sell products and services have been very IT-enabled. Internet-based business has become a major – if not a dominant or even the only – source of revenue for businesses across most industries.

IT as a Driver

For some companies IT provides truly an competitive edge. The use of technology to differentiate from others is part of everyone's DNA. People in these companies tend to be technologically savvy. They not only have an understanding what technology can do for them, but also they have a vision. You don't have to be a technology company, though, for IT to be a driver. You can be in retail and get the most out of technology to connect the supply and demand chain. You can be an insurance company and be a worldwide leader in building online communities around the insurances you sell. You can be in logistics and have the most advanced tracking and tracing capabilities. The core of the matter is that you have the tendency to see good use in any new technology you discover, and once in a while you invent a new technology of yourself. "Innovation" is the name of the game.

Philosophers in the Age of Enlightenment believed that the universe was running like a machine, a giant clock, and was adhering to certain rules. In order to understand the universe, all we had to do as human beings was take a rational look and figure out the rules. This is like peeling an onion, getting to the core of matter bit by bit, layer by layer. And not only the universe. The Enlightenment philosophers believed this to work for all areas in science, including social sciences, such as economy. If you understand the rules of reality, you have greater control over reality. No wonder the Age of Enlightenment was also called the Age of Reason. Western society has a long history believing in progress, science and technology, but it peaked again in the Age of Enlightenment after the dark ages and is still driving our thinking, particularly in IT, engineering and other technical areas. It is no surprise that if technology is your tool, then technology is what you believe to be the answer to your problems.

Technologists tend to believe in finding optimal solutions. Innovation is a way of lifting constraints and removing borders so next levels of business opportunities unfold. Within those levels and associated technologies, we can optimize until the next generation of technology presents itself, peeling yet another layer of the – perhaps eternal – onion.

Technology, therefore, is seen as a logical business

driver for competitive differentiation and for innovation.

However, as a single lens to look at innovation, IT as a driver may be a dangerous strategy as well. What about other approaches to business innovation? Competitive advantage might come from changing a company culture and emphasizing something as simple as friendliness (now that would be a good idea for lots of businesses). Innovation in the business model or in additional services might come from introducing a different shop floor layout. Product innovation may be in the quality of the assembly instructions. And so forth. In fact, one could create competitive advantage and innovation by using *less* technology in a product or customer service.

Furthermore, if "technology" is the default answer, there is always the pitfall of thinking that technology is per definition a good thing. The use of technology has behavioral consequences, not always for the better. Many a dinner party nowadays consists of a group of people each posting on Facebook that they're having a dinner party and checking their status every five minutes. We bring our music library to work and listen to our iPods, but don't communicate in the hallways anymore, killing all social interaction and, moreover, opportunities to help each other in the work that we do through serendipitous conversation.

Still, IT can be a powerful driver for strategic differentiation and innovation, but it comes in different shapes, depending on who is in the lead. That sounds logical if IT is in the lead in this strategy, after all technology is their core business. Still, this may not lead to the best results. Often we hear IT professionals ask themselves how to sell a new idea to the business or how to convince others of the value of the new idea. I wouldn't go as far as calling this strategy "hit and miss" because IT is more or less deciding the future of the business and trying to promote this in the business, but there might certainly be an element of accidental success involved. I wouldn't know in what percentage of IT organizations this is still a reality in this modern day and age, but a "technology push" strategy is certainly not uncommon.

What happens if business is in the lead, when managers are so IT savvy that they are in touch with all new technologies themselves all the time? It is quite possible that there simply will be no separate IT department. It will become an integral part of the business, most likely in some kind of matrix function, with technology professionals deeply permeated in every business function while at the same time reporting into some kind of centralized IT governance structure to ensure a uniform approach. Still, not all IT contributes to competitive differentiation. A large part is straightforward infrastructure and a commodity. Think of email, office applications, workplace management, standardized business applications and so forth. In this case, IT as a driver is most likely combined with IT as a utility, and is simply outsourced.

Every few years "the end of the CIO" is predicted, and the scenario of IT as an integral part of the business is painted. But this doesn't have to be the ideal situation. Take, for instance, organizations that are highly marketing-driven. They tend to have a strong marketing organization and a powerful chief marketing officer. Portfolio organizations that are very finance-oriented have a very strong finance function and a CFO that is on top of the business. These are all examples that map the situation where IT is not in the lead, and business is not in the lead. The mutual relationship is in the lead. There is a strong IT function, and there are highly technology savvy business departments. They work together all the time, inventing the future. This IT strategy enables true business transformation.

Your IT Strategy

There is a difference between an IT strategy and an IT philosophy. Strategies change over time; they describe the roadmap towards the goal. When circumstances change, a new strategy may be needed. An IT philosophy is less likely to change as it represents a fundamental belief in how the world works.

I described three distinct IT philosophies, namely IT as a utility, IT as an enabler and IT as a driver. When IT is a utility, it tries to be invisible and simply be there when needed. The goal is to make sure IT needs as little attention as possible so that all focus can be on business operations and business agility. IT as an enabler is a recipe for success when the organization is very business-case driven. This philosophy puts business performance improvement first. Then, all IT decisions are derived from that. IT as a driver is less concerned with the business case for improving current business operations. Ideally, it looks at creating tomorrow's business opportunity.

At the same time, we have seen there are multiple ways of creating and perceiving value. IT can be in the lead in any of these business philosophies. As the experts, it is their task to define what value technology can bring and evangelize that within the organization. The business can also be in the lead. They see IT as a powerful tool to achieve their goals. Lastly, neither of them are in the lead; they collaborate on the basis of being equals. Each discipline delivers critical skills and competences to deliver on the overall business strategy.

When we combine the three IT philosophies and the three ways of creating and perceiving value, we get a total of nine IT philosophies that organizations can have and that I have described while examining the IT philosophies.

	Business in the lead	IT in the lead	Relationship is leading
IT as a utility	Outsourcing	Infrastructure provider	Agile business building
IT as an enabler	Quick problem solving	Standardization	New business models
IT as a driver	Absorb IT	Technology push	Business transformation

Table 1: Nine IT Strategies

It is easy to criticize this table. For starters, it takes a very internally focused view. Isn't strategy all about competitive positioning? This is at least the school of thought personified by Michael Porter, the world's most influential professor in strategy. Structure follows strategy, as they say. A new strategy leads to a new style of organization. The table doesn't take any external change and any market position into account. It seems to advocate navel-gazing, and that cannot be right.

Then again, let's not judge that fast. There are other schools of thought in strategy. I don't see strategy as a purely analytical exercise. Strategy is not something that you can freely choose. A strategy can only be implemented successfully when it is authentic, when it fits the business. Certain strategies can only come out of certain organizations. It is almost inconceivable that Coca-Cola would ever relinquish its focus on its brand or that BMW will build the cheapest car in the world. Even surprising moves like fashion retail brand H&M asking famous fashion designers to contribute to the H&M collection fits to H&M's strategy on bringing fashion to the masses.

This is where I would like to focus. I don't think you can really "pick" a fundamental IT philosophy. You belong more or less to a certain school of thought, like philosophers do as well. It is unlikely that Immanuel Kant, who valued universal moral principles, would approve the pragmatist approach of "whatever works," or that Plato would nod in agreement with the postmodernists rejecting the idea of truth, or that the stoics would suddenly embracing hedonism.

I don't want to qualify any of the IT philosophies. IT as a utility, as an enabler and as a driver each are valid philosophies that present a comprehensive view on the value that IT brings. They can perfectly exist next to each other, each offering a different look at the world. The question is not whether they are "good" philosophies or not, but whether they fit the organization.

Does this mean that as an organization you don't have

any strategic room? That you are bound by your own philosophy and can't escape from it? That is also not the case.

Organizations can radically change philosophy, probably just not with the same set of people. Moving from IT as a utility to IT as a driver (or vice versa) requires a different skill set, a different communication between the various disciplines in the business and, frankly, a fundamentally different outlook on how to approach information technology. Really changing IT philosophy comes at a price. It requires an organizational reboot, almost starting from scratch. Investments from the past may not meet the new business case, and all the decisions and behaviors that were successful in the past may very well now lead to failure.

Having said that, having one philosophy doesn't mean you can completely ignore the others. Like some philosophers have in common that they discuss the meaning of life, the commonality in IT philosophies is that they describe the value of IT. Just in a different way. Even if you want to argue that IT has no value, you still need to understand and define the term value before you can deny it.

Furthermore, the philosophies have some interdependency. As innovative as you want to be, there is always a large part of utility. Focusing on IT operational excellence doesn't mean you can close your eyes to innovation or to expressing the value of IT in terms of business value. To return to Treacy and Wiersema's value disciplines, which match so well with the three IT philosophies, you need to be sufficient in all of them, but need to really excel in one in order to be successful.

So the three IT philosophies are equal, and I didn't qualify one as better than the others. However, I do believe that the three ways of creating and perceiving value can be qualified. I do believe that one party taking the lead, whether it is IT or the business, in both cases leads to suboptimal results. My descriptions of the IT strategies and the table suggested that as well. If IT is in the lead, there is a technology push, a generic infrastructure, or a strong tendency towards standardization. Wonderful, but to what end? The answer to that is not clear in any of the three cases. If the business is in the lead, the goals are not the issue. But do you get everything out of it? Outsourcing companies have their own goals, and quick problem solving rarely leads to well-architected and repeatable solutions. Absorbing IT may be the best option in this scenario.

However, if the various disciplines treat each other as equals, each representing unique and necessary skill sets, the business starts to move. If IT is a utility, you can create world-class agility. If IT is an enabler, new business models keep getting the most out of your products and services; and if IT is a driver, there is an opportunity to reinvent yourself.

So work towards putting the relationship between business and IT in the middle with either with no one in the lead, or with the person who happens to have the right skills for a certain project in the lead. Where the business does not hand over specifications to IT, but is in it all the way. Where IT does not use the term "internal customer." All share the same customers, and they are out there in the marketplace.

At least that's my philosophy.

In Search
of Wisdom

The Oracle of Delphi once labeled Socrates the wisest of all. Socrates was perplexed, since he didn't consider himself wise. Socrates set out on a quest to prove the oracle wrong, asking questions to the people in Athens he thought of as wise: notables, judges, city administrators and so forth. To their dismay, his probing questions revealed that these so-called wise people did not have much wisdom; they could not answer Socrates' questions in a satisfactory manner. Socrates came to the conclusion that if he did possess any wisdom, it was in the realization that at least he was convinced he knew little, in contrast to all the high-placed so-called wise people.

Socrates' smart questions, and the effect they had on the youth in Athens, annoyed the authorities so much that they put him on trial. Even confronted with the choice between exile and death, Socrates kept questioning and challenging the court. He was sentenced to death.

Was Socrates the wisest of all because he valued his way of thinking more than life itself? Or did the guy just not know when to stop, showing there is a thin line between independent critical thinking and plain stubbornness?

Philosophy literally means "the love for wisdom." Philosophers, therefore, are people who have a love for wisdom. But that doesn't necessarily mean they display characteristics or behaviors we usually associate with wisdom. Nietzsche went mad, Confucius couldn't get a job, Machiavelli was thrown out of office, and others affiliated themselves with questionable regimes.

What is Wisdom?

Wisdom proves to be a confusing subject of discussion and analysis, riddled with paradox. Wisdom is based on having a certain amount of knowledge of things, but it applies most to areas of uncertainty, such as future consequences of actions, or the consequences of decisions on others. A wise person can draw on significant knowledge, but keeps questioning everything. Wisdom means knowing what to do and when to do it, but it is equally about what not to do, and when not to do it. A wise person is deeply grounded in practice and has seen it all, yet stands above all. Wisdom means having a deep understanding of human emotions, but requires emotional detachment to keep things clear. Wisdom is usually associated with mastering self-reflection, but is mostly used as a label for people to turn to for advice.

Highly confusing. It is easy to list some wise people, like Gandhi, Mandela, Einstein, and even Yoda from the film *Star Wars*. But what it is that makes them wise?

The most common definition is that wisdom is a deep understanding and realizing of people, things, events or situations, resulting in the ability to choose or act or inspire to consistently produce the optimum results with a minimum of time, energy or thought. What is nice about this definition is that it introduces a continuous tension between two forces – a maximum of results, with a minimum of effort. The more you achieve with less effort, the wiser you are. The problem I have with the definition is that it's an almost mechanistic view of wisdom, searching for an optimum. This definition must have its roots in the age of reason. With a little bit of effort, though, we can infer more from this definition.

Given that both forces are continuously shifting, the definition also suggests some kind of fragile equilibrium, a careful balance. You can't stop investing in wisdom because the factors it depends on (results and effort) continuously change. This makes total sense to me, and it sounds much more human, too. Still, there seems to be something missing. If wisdom requires an inquisitive mind that never stops questioning and wondering, the price for that is a certain lack of efficiency. Exploration comes with dead ends and some delays based on thinking things through one more time or considering another angle. I'd like to see a definition that is less efficient in nature, and more about effectiveness.

Postmodern Problems

The postmodern definition currently prevailing isn't much help either. It says that wisdom is defined much more by the perceiver than by the source. In this sense, wisdom is nothing more than a social label. Wisdom is the concept derived from the examples that you have seen of people who are called wise. This pure, empirical view based on observation is very fashionable in social sciences that currently are very affected by neuroscience. Neuroscience is very influential in psychology, in areas related to decision theory, and there are even field called neuroeconomics and neuromarketing. Neuroscience also affects philosophy (particularly epistemology), because it focuses on how the human brain processes information, stores knowledge, makes decisions, and comes to action. In short, the brain is seen as a huge pattern recognition engine that works largely inductively. This means that the human brain creates concepts based on examples. The rule is derived from observations. Therefore, a cow is nothing else than an instance of similar things that we are taught to call cow. Wisdom is the behavior of those we call wise.

This view, true as it may be, is utterly useless when it comes to figuring out what wisdom means. It is the death trap for defining any concept. What this line of thinking does is shift all attributes of an object (all the things that describe it) to attributes of an observation. This opens the door for no truth in anything whatsoever – your attributes can be different than mine, but no better than mine. Truth has become opinion. If you try to prove me wrong, that is simply your opinion.

Much of the discussion is about opinion already. For instance, Confucius could easily be considered the pro-totypical wise man. A pupil once asked him (and I am paraphrasing loosely here) what he should do with new lessons learned. Should he find an opportunity to test them immediately? Confucius responded, "Not as long as your elder brother and father are alive." (He meant the pupil should follow due process and follow the hierarchy before trying something new.) Later, another pupil asked the same question, and Confucius answered, "Of course! Right away." Obviously, Confucius' other pupils pointed out their master's inconsistent answers. Confucius then explained that the first pupil needed a bit of restraint, because he was so eager, and the second pupil needed encouragement, as he was a bit behind. Confucius took a broader perspective and weighed specific circumstances in his answer.

Immanuel Kant (1724–1804) seems to state the opposite. He felt our decisions should be guided by the categorical imperative. In short, "Act only according to that maxim whereby you can, at the same time, will that it should become a universal law." This means there are no circumstances that would affect your decisions. You need to do the right thing regardless, based on universal principles. For instance, it is *always* wrong to lie, to steal or to kill. If you lie, you contradict the reliability of language, and then we cannot rely on any form of communication. Therefore, *a priori*, it is wrong to lie. Wisdom, then, would be the ability to act according to these universal laws. Again, we are not much further in our quest to understand wisdom.

An Analysis of Wisdom

Still, the postmodern view does allow us to analyze the concept of wisdom. The most obvious type of analysis would be to look at any attributes we can find associated with wisdom. As these attributes are not connected to wisdom itself, but to the perception of wisdom, it seems all we need to do is find the attributes that are shared by enough people, so we can induce a general picture. Wise people are humble and serene, have a deep sense of self-reflection and see things as they are, and so forth. Unfortunately, the analytical view isn't much help, because you will probably find many attributes that seem to contradict each other. For example, wisdom requires deep knowledge, but also a high level of detachment. A wise person has many years of experience, but still questions everything. Wise people are consulted for their insight into someone else's position, not for their own self-reflection. Wisdom is as much about doing things as it is about not doing them, and so forth. It is going to be hard to find a sufficiently shared view.

Even if it would be possible to find such a shared view, it wouldn't help. Is everyone who has experience and a certain level of intelligence wise? I don't think so. Is everyone who questions everything, has serenity, and is self-reflective considered wise? Again, the answer would have to be no. If we add more attributes, such as knowing when to do something, and applying a minimum of effort, would that complete the picture? The answer is still no. There obviously is some kind of X-factor that sits in between having or displaying certain characteristics and being wise.

Synthesis – Not Analysis

This typical style of analysis is clearly a dead end; it doesn't catch the X-factor, that turns out to be the essence of wisdom. We need a style of thinking that is less analytic and more – what I call – synthetic of nature. Analytical thinking is what we are taught in business. The simplest definition of analysis is to break something (such as an object or a concept) into smaller parts to understand its workings. Synthesis is the opposite of analysis. It is the process of fusing different things into a new object or concept, creating synergy. Synthesis is not about finding differences (an analytical concept), but about reconciling differences.

Let's try synthetic thinking to reconcile some of the different and conflicting aspects of wisdom. What is it that having vast experience while remaining curious have in common? What connects emotional insight and detachment? How do self-reflection and giving good advice relate? When do you have to bend, and when you do hold your ground?

"Context" comes to mind as an overarching principle. Context is the set of circumstances or facts that surround a particular event, situation, and so forth. In other words, context is everything that affects the object of study, but not the object of study itself. In fact, American writer, historian and philosopher Will Durant (1885-1981) even based his definition of wisdom on it. Ideally, Durant states, wisdom is total perspective – seeing an object, event or idea in all its pertinent relationships. Baruch Spinoza (1632-1677), Dutch philosopher, defined wisdom as seeing things *sub specie eternitatis*, in view of eternity; Durant suggested defining it as seeing things *sub specie totius*, in view of the whole.

The moment you have total perspective, you know when to do what. You know when to speak and when to remain silent, when to bend and when to hold your ground, when to rely on your experience and when to see the world through the eyes of a child. Perspective is gained by being aware of what "frame" or point of view you use to see the world, and by putting yourself in someone else's shoes as well. In other words, by applying multiple frames you get a more complete perspective, and come up – like Confucius – with a situational response. Situational thinking and awareness of context are very close: If you understand the context of the matter, you can pick the right approach. Experience helps you learn how to be effective using multiple approaches.

But this is not true synthetic thinking... yet. There are more powerful ways to act on total perspective. Seeking synthesis means not simply making an either/or choice, but finding a way to do and/and or, even better, through/through. You can gain far more power by being humble, like Gandhi. You can give better advice to others, because you can detach from your own frame. In other words, you can understand others by better understanding yourself. Synthetic thinking proves to be helpful when being confronted with conflicting points of view, like in the attributes of (perceived) wisdom.

There is some truth to the famous quote by F. Scott Fitzgerald: "The test of a first-rate intelligence is the ability to hold two opposing ideas in the mind at the same time and still retain the ability to function." However, I think this describes wisdom, not intelligence.

Rise Above Your Subject Matter

Doing the right thing at the right time under the right circumstances is all about context. But it is hard to see the context of any matter from within. An expert carpenter sees carpentry solutions for most problems. A seasoned politician sees laws and regulations as the means to affect society. A software vendor's sales representative sees a software package as the magic bullet, while the vendor-independent consultant sees a project as the way to go. Context, beginning with the borders of what you know, only becomes visible if you step outside your area of expertise – more precisely, if you rise above your subject matter.

If wisdom is seeing things in total perspective, including all context, and the ability to reconcile conflicting perspectives, then this is my proposed addition to the mix: Wisdom requires rising above your subject matter.

"Rising" means there is a continuous process. A wise person is never done. There is always more to learn and other points of view to explore. A person can't have experience and display wisdom in every field of expertise. Most people develop according to what is often called the T-model. They develop a certain specialty and become an expert over time, then spread their wings, realizing that other areas of expertise are based on similar concepts, of which they can have a good working knowledge. You can have experience in a field without displaying wisdom, but a wise person wouldn't comment on areas he or she feels uncomfortable about. The phrase "your subject matter" also suggests that wisdom itself is contextual. For instance, someone can be remarkably wise for his or her age, having perspective of certain areas, but not have the maturity and experience in other, more grown-up matters. Only if you detach yourself from your areas of expertise can you see its limitations, relations to adjacent areas and similarities to other fields.

If wisdom is a continuous process, it suggests that wisdom is relative. I don't think anyone suddenly becomes wise. It is a gradual process that is never finished. At the same time, wisdom can also be seen as an absolute state. How do you measure wisdom and how do you compare wisdom? Was Socrates wiser than Confucius? You can't really say who is wise, wiser and wisest. Again, we need to apply synthetic thinking. How can wisdom be relative and absolute at the same time? One way of reconciling the two is to see wisdom as an attitude. This attitude, a typical style of thinking, can be fairly constant and applied over and over. Wisdom, then, is not about knowing the best answer, but knowing how to get there.

So ... we are a little bit further in our understanding of wisdom, but we still haven't touched on the business relevance of this discussion. I will do that in my next article.

What's the point?

Studying wisdom is kind of depressing. Many have tried to capture the essence of wisdom in the last 2,500 years, but there is still some mystery to wisdom. We don't get to the core of the matter, and I didn't expect to achieve that in the process of writing this article.

To make matters worse, wisdom seems to be a road to nowhere. The more you are on your way to wisdom, the more you will start denying it. While others may call you wise, wisdom tells you there's not much you know for sure. Socrates didn't consider himself wise, except perhaps in the sense that he realized he didn't possess any wisdom.

There is a story that in the 7th century B.C., there was a golden tripod to be given to the wisest of all. It was offered first to Thales, one of the seven sages of Greece, but he refused to accept. In turn, the golden tripod then was offered to each of the other six sages – Cleobulus, Solon, Chilon, Bias, Pittacus and Periander. None accepted.

Based on 2,500 years of observation, I guess the only thing we can truly say about wisdom is that when you claim you have it, you don't. Unfortunately, it doesn't work the other way around. The realization that you are not wise doesn't automatically make you wise. How to make sense out of that?

Perhaps this is a very good reason to study wisdom. For any knowledge worker, business analyst or strategist, it can be a humbling experience to take on an impossible subject. At first glance, wisdom seems like a pretty straightforward concept. We can point out people we consider wise, and we have an intuitive understanding of what it means. But the more we apply analytical thinking to it, the further away we get from the core of the matter. It is good to realize that there are limits to what we can analyze and truly understand. In fact, this realization is a good start on the path to wisdom.

Thomas of Aquino (1225-1274), an Italian theologian and philosopher, considered wisdom the father of all virtues. This may appeal to professionals in any field to grow from a practitioner who understands the "know what" to an expert with a grip on the "know how" to the wise person who masters the "know why."

This is another good reason to build an appreciation for wisdom. Studying philosophy helps you to get to the "know why." However, the road to wisdom is not trivial. Being a lover of wisdom – the literal meaning of philosopher – doesn't necessarily mean you are wise. Not even the great philosophers are wise per se. Take, for instance, German philosopher Georg Wilhem Friedrich Hegel (1770-1831), who described the history of philosophy through a three-step continuous process: thesis-antithesis-synthesis. The thesis is a situation in time, the antithesis represents the reaction to that situation, and the synthesis is the reconciliatory force that unites the thesis and antithesis. After that, the synthesis turns into the thesis, and the dialectic approach starts all over. Hegel argued that each dialectic step takes us closer to an optimal situation. Applied to politics, Hegel found that the Prussian government system in which he lived represented the perfect and final synthesis. Even Hegel was not able to overcome his own paradigm and create a total perspective. In fact, we are all a product of our age. The life and times of most philosophers has shaped their thinking.

The megatrends in business and IT also provide a reason to explore the concept of wisdom. *Big data* is the mantra in data and information management. Managers are fed by *business intelligence* systems. Business processes are quickly becoming more *knowledge intensive*. Business operations need to be *optimized*. There is a clear relationship in these trends; they represent a hierarchy or value chain often referred to as data-information-knowledge.

Let's explore this a little further. Sometimes we hear "the numbers speak for themselves," but this is rarely the case. Data in the form of measurements do not mean a lot by themselves. If I ask how business is going and the CFO responds, "42," what does that mean?[1] It becomes meaningful only when the context is provided, such as 42 million in revenue, a 42% increase in profit, or 42 new product features launched. In other words, context is needed to transform data to information. But it is not useful yet. Subsequently, it requires knowledge, experience and intelligence to make information actionable.

This is where we are now in the maturity curve of IT. We use social media to share knowledge and experience; and if we collaborate to include multiple angles to solve a problem or create a new strategy, we can come up with more intelligent courses of action. The old idea of knowledge management systems from the 1980s and 1990s is re-emerging, making use of all kinds of semantic technologies in which we store this collective intelligence from multiple viewpoints so it can be reapplied and decision making can even be automated to some extent. Data

---

1 This is in reference to The Hitchhiker's Guide to the Galaxy, a book by Douglas Adams that tells a story of a huge computer that is built to answer the "question of life, the universe and everything." However, when the computer finally responds with "42," humanity is puzzled. This can't be correct, what does it mean, they ask the computer. The computer recomputes the answer, confirms its correctness and suggests that if the people don't understand the answer, maybe they didn't really understand their question in the first place. There is a deep truth in that. The question itself is the first context to the answer. "How's business doing?" is indeed not the best phrased of all questions.

mining has become both powerful and scalable so we can detect patterns and act upon them in a much smarter way.

So, if the need for information guides what data we need to track and intelligent questions guide what information we need, what guides the intelligence that we possess and that is so greatly enhanced by technology?

Wisdom.

With so many technological constraints being lifted, intelligence is not the boundary condition anymore.[2] Wisdom provides the guardrails to intelligence and knowledge. Wisdom helps us distinguish right from wrong. It provides a moral compass. The central question in business and technology has moved from "How do we do things?" to "What should we do, why should we do that, and when would be a good moment?"

If you work for a pharmaceutical company and you perform advanced data mining on clinical data, there may be many answers you will find to questions that you didn't even ask. What are the consequences of those answers? If you find a correlation between elements of lifestyle and certain medical conditions, should you inform patients? The moral consequences of saying "yes" are as unsurmountable as saying "no."

If you work for Google, Twitter or Facebook, and you mine online behavior, how far can you go in targeted advertising and create an online profile of someone that starts to lead a life of its own (chew a while on the expression "lead a life of its own," and imagine how literal this could be in the digital world)? We are in the middle of discovering that, through all kinds of scandals, painful lessons are learned.

If you are a regulator, and through advanced economic modeling you see realistic scenarios in which a certain bank will not survive a sudden possible turn in the market, should you warn the public of that? You can't undo

---

2 If you allow me the cynical observation, intelligence has become as borderless as stupidity.

the knowledge, but it is uncertain the scenario will indeed happen. If you warn the market, you create a self-fulfilling prophecy; if you don't, you may be held accountable for your lack of action later on.

Should threats made on Twitter by teenagers be taken seriously, given their global reach? How can a business intelligence system help you make a decision, and when to make it? Can you tell a data mining tool what you would not like to find? Is WikiLeaks a blessing or a curse to the world? How far can we go with cameras in the street and intelligent software identifying potentially disruptive behavior of people walking there? To what extent should health care providers and associated insurance companies have access to a patient's integrated medical file? How far should we go in automated decision making regarding loans, permits, grants, benefits, fines and so forth, without a basic understanding of the social context of the applicant?

It seems we have insufficient perspective. We are in dire need of wisdom.

So, Where Do I Stand?

I have freely expressed my opinions on philosophy and IT throughout the book, and it turns out these opinions are not unique. In philosophical terms, I learned that I am a *liberal communitarianist*. Hold on, don't call in the cops yet – this technical term may not exactly be what it could suggest in a modern political connotation. It is not left-wing, it is not right-wing. Communitarianists first and foremost believe people are social beings. People are born, grow up and die as part of a society. Our frame of reference, beliefs and values are based on where we live – we call that culture. Communitarianists frown on pure individualism. They don't see the appeal of a society in which everyone is supposed to take care of themselves, leading to an optimum well-being for all, when considering it on a macro scale.

Translating this to business, I see more leverage in the stakeholder model. Stakeholders have needs that we need to address. In return they have unique contributions for our success as well. Investing in their success leads to returns that we could never achieve by ourselves. If we invest in our neighborhood and the people we work with, it pays back. This is not a zero-sum game, but a win-win situation. Well-being is not a scarce good that we need to compete for.

A cursory glance at the typical large enterprise proves my point. Managers compete for budgets and resources, and feel responsible for their domain. The result, as many of us can attest, is suboptimal: lots of small parts that don't align very well. If managers felt responsible for the whole of the organization and we had more collaborative incentives and control systems in place, every organizational unit would not only know what it contributes to the success of the organization, but also to the success of the other parts of the organization. One step beyond, including business partners and other parties in the industry value chain, stakeholder thinking leads to what is often called a *business ecosystem*.

Communitarians don't believe in top-down rules coming from governing institutions. They'd rather see communities overseeing themselves. I don't believe in big government; I believe it is the task of the government to enable society to organize itself. A popular term in the UK that describes this approach is "big society." Translated to the business world, stakeholder thinking would lead to – forgive the pun – big business.

I don't believe business performs at its best under heavy rules-based regulation. Compliance costs are through the roof and lead to tick-box systems. Sticking to the rules doesn't mean you're positively contributing to (or at least not extracting value from) society. Principles-based regulations, also known as comply-or-explain, force organizations to explain why they have made certain choices and be transparent about them. If stakeholders feel this is not enough or is not what they consider right, organizations isolate themselves. This is a much richer and organic approach, leading to a much more resilient business ecosystem.

Communitarianism equals hippie ideas? Naive? Hardly. Business has always been this way. In medieval times, the different guilds that organized the various trades in a city would also be responsible for guarding the city walls. This would increase safety, leading to what we today call increased consumer confidence. This would lead to more trade, more prosperity, and a bigger investment in safety. Business was small, and this has changed in the industrial age. Globalization has led to much higher prosperity, but in the process large enterprise has disconnected itself from society, calling itself amoral. But with more than one-third of the largest economic entities in the world being corporations, not countries, business cannot be amoral. Business does affect our quest for the good life. Business needs to rediscover its close ties to society, which is more than maximizing shareholder returns.

Communitarianism equals old-fashioned thinking? Reminiscing old times? I don't think so. In fact, community thinking and peer structures are the central paradigm in the 2.0 world. Generation Y doesn't look to the school principal, senior management or any other authority for answers; they consult each other and build a collective opinion. Twitter has started complete revolutions. In fact, technology has greatly democratized society on a much more direct level than ever before. With our smartphones and social media, we have technology powerful enough to check on our government at all levels. The police can't misbehave, decision making in government institutions is openly questioned and influenced, and politics can be more directly influenced as well. Translated to business, in the 2.0 world, a single person with a good idea can build a global business with virtually no upfront investment. Specialist work can be outsourced to other parties, crossing multiple borders and time zones. As technology evangelists often claim, through open-source initiatives and crowdsourcing, collectives create innovation that large vertically structured organizations can't even dream of.

In all honesty, the communitarian view has some serious challenges. Communities can become very forceful and determine our identity. This has been the case with all types of communities, earthly and religious. People need to be able to fulfill their dreams and live their lives through self-determination within the communities they choose to be part of. This is not without commitment. One can only expect community support when there is a form of community contribution. The relationship needs to be reciprocal for communities to last.

But we cannot allow every community to come up with their own laws. There needs to be a certain set of guarantees for liberty across society; this is why most countries have a constitution. Communities have to be protected so they can thrive freely, but citizens also must be protected from communities going overboard and endangering their freedom and liberty.

That's why I take the liberal approach to community thinking. Citizens shouldn't be "locked into" a certain community; there needs to be an opt-out. Furthermore, one limitation that technology did take away is that a community necessarily have geographical borders. In the

2.0 world, we are part of many communities, each contributing a little bit to our identity.

That's where I stand.

Recommended
Reading

Okay, I'll admit it. I used Wikipedia to look up things for *Socrates Reloaded*. Wikipedia is good at and meant for getting a first impression of a subject to see if it is worth further studying. I also used Google, searching for popular and academic pages and papers that helped clarify complex topics and arguments. Who doesn't? The moment some part of this book captures your attention, these are great ways to start learning more, as you probably do daily in your own work and activities.

What is missing from Wikipedia, Google and most other web resources is a rich context that makes you understand the bigger picture. How can trends in philosophy be explained as a reaction to other trends? How did the various philosophers influence each other? What place do certain philosophies have as a product of their time in history? These are not questions that are easily answered by browsing around. They require richer sources.

Following is a very small selection of sources I used in writing this book. I selected the ones that would be the most interesting for those readers who'd like to delve a little deeper. From there, dear reader, I am sure you will find your own way through a lifetime of learning.

Stanford Encyclopedia of Philosophy and the Internet Encyclopedia of Philosophy

These are the best Web resource that I have found.[1] They are comprehensive, both in breadth and in depth. As there are many contributing entries, some are easier to read than others. But overall, this has become my first go-to place if I want to understand a new topic in philosophy.

Justice – Michael Sandel

Harvard University's most well-known philosophy professor, Michael Sandel, has put a complete series of lectures on YouTube.[2] These lectures are full of humor, student interaction and amazing insights. Watching all of

---

1 http://plato.stanford.edu/ and http://www.iep.utm.edu/

them helped me prepare for a number of themes in the book. Most of what is discussed in the series is also part of Sandel's book, called *Justice*. This book is one of the few in-depth philosophy books I read with contemporary examples, and it is really fun to read.

The History of Philosophy – Brian Magee

Probably the best place to start to get a quick overview of the complete history of philosophy is Brian Magee's book, *The History of Philosophy*. Abundantly illustrated, it captures the essence of most schools of thought, from the old Greeks and Chinese to twentieth century philosophy.

History of Western Philosophy – Bertrand Russell

However, if you are in for some serious reading, the best overview that I have read so far is Bertrand Russell's History of Western Philosophy. Russell, a renowned 20th century philosopher himself, argues that if the old philosophers claimed universal truth on a number of issues, it is perfectly okay to challenge those truths with the knowledge and progress of today. Russell doesn't hold back and doesn't accept the "you have to see the work of the old philosophers in the light of the world in which they lived back then" excuse. As a famous philosopher himself, Russell presents both a thorough overview and takes position himself. He has skin in the game.

Philosophy for Dummies – Tom Morris

Don't laugh. This is a very good general overview of philosophy. For dummies? Hardly. It takes extreme skill to describe various philosophical schools of thought in plain and simple terms, without losing the essence of them. A definite must-read. It has been an inspiration for me to learn how to boil down complex discussions to the essence.

---

2 http://www.youtube.com/watch?v=kBdfcR-8hEY or http://www.justiceharvard.org/

Moral Theory, An Introduction – Mark Timmons

In studying philosophy, it won't take you long to identify the topics that resonate most with you. For me, the topics were ethics and moral theory as bits and pieces of political philosophy. Not the easiest of books to read, *Moral Theory* provides a thorough overview of all schools of thought in this area.

Contemporary Political Philosophy – Will Kymlicka

Kymlicka's book is considered the standard overview on political philosophy. Again, it's not the most entertaining of reads, but it does provide a good overview. Kymlicka focuses on comparing and contrasting different schools of thought, instead of describing them independent from each other.

Examined Lives – James Miller

We are all the product of our time. Even some of the great philosophers had trouble overcoming the shortcomings of their own paradigms. For instance, Hegel reasoned that the 18th century Preusian form of government truly presented the ideal state. James Miller doesn't describe the various philosophies in different ages; he describes the lives of the philosophers against the backdrop of the time and place where they lived. The title is a very appropriate reference to a famous quote from Socrates: "The unexamined life is not worth living."

Primary Literature

Most of my recommendations here are secondary literature. Books that describe other books. Yes, I do have Kant's collected works in my bookshelf, but honestly, that's the only book I didn't really read. Some philosophers pride themselves in their work being hard to understand. According to some, philosophy is really only for those who are smart enough to learn a completely new jargon. Jargon may be very efficient in communicating in a very precise way, but I don't buy that argument. If you claim to have important contributions to make to "the good life" (an important topic in philosophy), then you should be willing and able to allow as many people as possible to benefit from it. Fortunately, some primary literature is very accessible.

The Art of War – Sun Tzu

Not really a book that has a story line or a clear logic in argument, *The Art of War* is more of a collection of short lessons and statements. Very relevant for today's business nevertheless.

The Prince – Machiavelli

Who would think a 16th century book could be an entertaining read. Machiavelli's *The Prince* certainly is. Unlike most other philosophers, Machiavelli doesn't describe how things should be, but how they work in practice. It seems many lessons of power and leadership apply as much in the 16th century as they do now.

The Republic – Plato

Most of Plato's work is written in the form of dialogue, often featuring his master Socrates. It is unclear if Plato is putting his own words in Socrates' mouth, or is truly representing Socrates' view. Many English translations have copious footnotes and elaborate side descriptions to explain what Plato is telling us through the dialogues, giving both the pleasure of the dialogue and a thorough background.

If you are in search of wisdom, I am afraid none of these books will provide the definitive answer. But that shouldn't stop you. Starting with one or a few of these books can be a humbling experience. They may teach you how you can stand on the shoulders of giants. They may tell you where you stand so you know that your point of view is not unique. It is probably discussed (and rejected by others) on a much deeper level than you could do yourself. These books may also greatly help you framing, contextualizing and sharpening your thoughts so you can better reflect. And that may very well be the beginning of wisdom.

About the Author

Frank Buytendijk's professional background in strategy, performance management and organizational behavior gives him a strong perspective across many domains in business and IT. A former Gartner Research VP and a seasoned IT executive, Frank is an exceptional speaker at conferences all over the world, known for his original point of views, funny observations and his slightly provocative style. More down to earth, his daughter once described it as "My daddy sits in airplanes, stands on stages, and tells jokes."

Frank is a visiting fellow at Cranfield University School of Management, a regular guest lecturer at London School of Economics, and a TDWI fellow.

Earlier books by Frank include Performance Leadership (McGraw-Hill, September 2008) and Dealing with Dilemmas (Wiley & Sons, August 2010).

www.frankbuytendijk.com
@FrankBuytendijk

CPSIA information can be obtained at www.ICGtesting.com
Printed in the USA
LVOW04s1936090615

441778LV00035B/1313/P